The Ghost Towns of 174

Willie Davis

AuthorHouse
Bloomington, Indiana

AuthorHouse™
1663 Liberty Drive
Bloomington, IN 47403
www.authorhouse.com
Phone: 1-800-839-8640

Published by AuthorHouse 4/27/2012

ISBN: 978-1-4685-6676-5 (sc)
ISBN: 978-1-4685-6677-2 (e)

Library of Congress Control Number: 2012905263

This book is printed on acid-free paper.

For Aubrey, Kaylee, Alaina, Caleb, and Ben

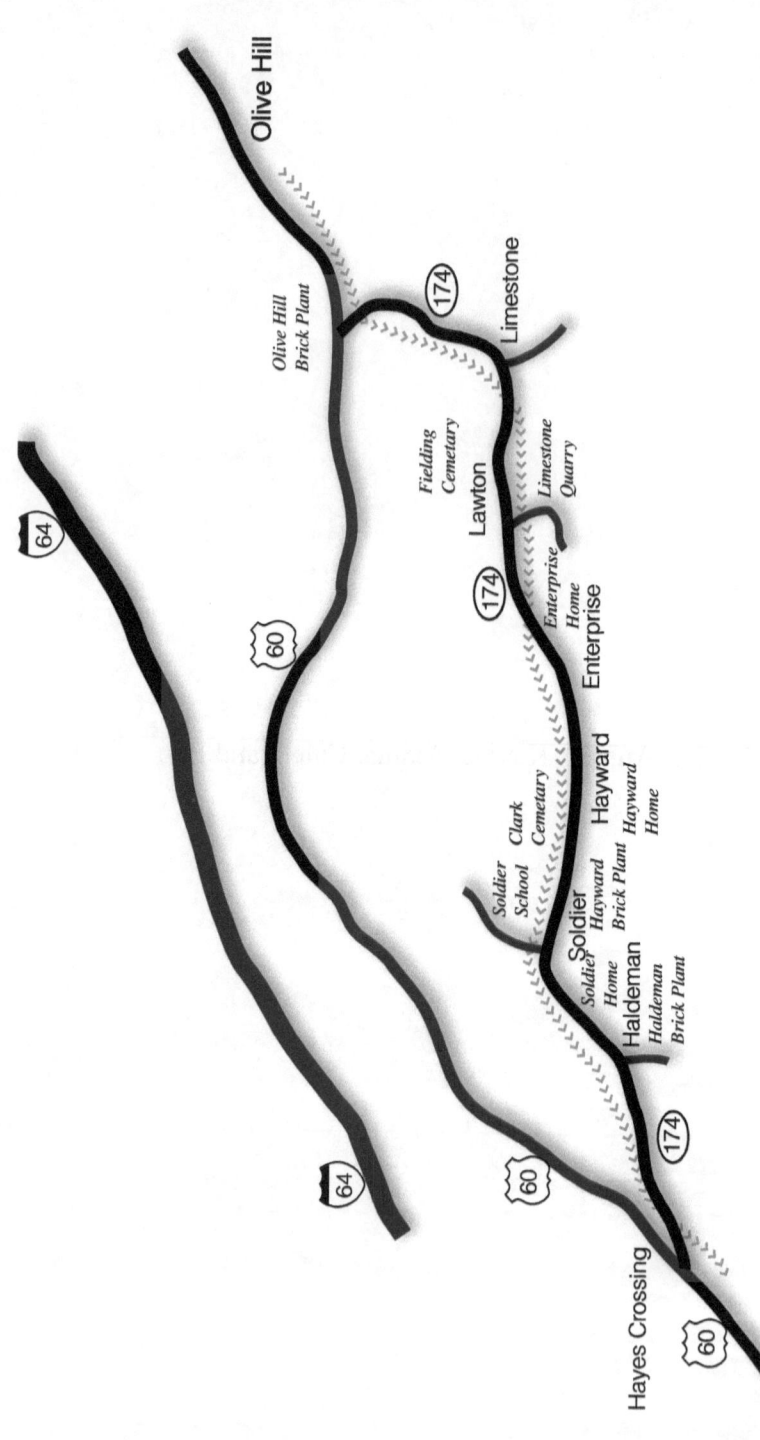

Olive Hill

Olive Hill
Brick Plant

174

Limestone

64

Fielding
Cemetary

Lawton

Limestone
Quarry

60

174

Enterprise
Home

Enterprise

Clark
Cemetary

Soldier
School

Hayward

Hayward
Home

Soldier
Hayward
Brick Plant

Soldier
Home

Soldier

Haldeman

Haldeman
Brick Plant

64

60

174

Hayes Crossing

60

Morehead

Contents

Contents

Introduction

Each one of us lives in our own private world.

Although biologically we are all similar, our difference lies in how we perceive the world around us. Our individual senses process our personal experiences and incoming information into stored mental images. These mental images mesh together in our brain and form our feelings and opinions, which are called perceptual realities. Therefore, the color of the sky in your world, in all probability, is different than mine.

As an individual, your perceptual realities are yours alone. Never be fearful of expressing them as they come from the highest source on earth – you! We build our realities from scratch and only change them when new information is significant enough to crash our ongoing mental image party. Advertisers and politicians are forever wanting in.

I have been proven guilty over the years of creating something new and interesting enough to change someone's perceptual reality. My hope is that this book is another one of those times – especially for my grandchildren.

I have five grandchildren who are geographically scattered. I've watched over the years as each grow and paint their sky in their own way. I realized a while back that my grandchildren are like a lot of today's children, in that they know little about their family history beyond their grandparents. Their world is a profusion of technology, mixed with "today's experiences" and a deluge of 24/7 information – void of any ancestral meaning or understanding.

The truth is our heritage is a part of our DNA. It's a link to our past. I have learned that life is a group sport, and my grandchildren's sky will have a black hole if they don't become familiar with one of the most important groups in their life, their family.

They are still too young to ask, "How did I come to be here?" One day they will ask that question. When they do, this ancestral world I've created from my perceptual realities will hopefully help strengthen their perceptual realities and carry them through the tough times they are sure to face.

As I checked old family dates, plowed through old family pictures, and deciphered twenty-year-old hand-written perceptual realities from Mom, I realized that other family members might find merit to this family world I was creating.

In addition to some wonderful stories of sacrifice, accomplishment, heartache, and love inside my family, I discovered information about Carter County and Kentucky that I didn't know as a child. I sure there are a lot of ex-Carter Countians who didn't know how important Carter County was in propelling this nation forward. This information for them might raise an eyebrow or two.

Unfortunately, there is a downside when an author tries to transform real life into art – the truth, as perceptually seen by others, is assaulted. Many people believe that the opposite of something true is false. I, on the other hand, believe the opposite of a truth can be another truth. Some people will question whether incidents in these pages really happened that way. Others will be glad to set the record straight where I obviously "got it wrong." While a name or two may be misspelled, a date or sequence may be a little out of whack, this book is my perceptual reality, and it is written with only the best intentions. Offending the reader was not one of my goals.

Some pushback will probably come from my title, "The Ghost Towns of 174." Obviously there are still people living in the six communities described here. However, those people cannot deny that life on that 11-mile stretch of road is a mere shadow of decades past. In the world I have described in this book, the six Ghost Towns are not defined as abandoned, but as an economic shell of times past. The term Ghost Town is an expression of art that is intended to stir the imagination, not pass judgment on current residents.

The big picture in this book is simple. I was born in 1947 in Olive Hill, Kentucky. My younger brother, Harlan, was born in 1949. Our lives, and the lives of our parents Harlan Davis and Ruth Hall, their parents, brothers, sisters, nieces, and nephews, were connected to a small 11-mile stretch of State Route 174 between Olive Hill and Morehead. I was 12 and Harlan was 10 when our family of four moved to Mansfield to begin anew. These are my perceptions about life along Route 174 and the people who lived there before that move.

The story here identifies four generations of my family. I briefly travel down the rabbit hole of time, talk a little about Kentucky's great out-migration, Carter County's service to this country, the roads and communities that shaped my early life, and the Davis and Hall families – who they were and how their generation helped forge this nation.

But, watch out: as you read, you run the risk of being affected by my perceptual reality and might, perhaps, alter your own.

A reading note...

Before her death in 1994, Mom penned some thoughts about the people she loved and some of her childhood and adult memories. I inserted some of her perceptual realities into mine. You'll see them printed like this, smaller italicized type centered on the page. They are quite revealing.

I Remember...

by Ruth Davis

Generations and Historical Cycles

Cornflakes and Slinkies

Ask any student for the least favorite subject in school, and history is sure to be among the top. Many of today's youth believe history is a bowl of cornflakes, directionless random events thrown into the bowl of time. Why should they care whether World War II was fought in the 1940s or the 1840s? The present and the future is what's important, not those dates that students memorize simply to pass the next test.

Random History

In addition, today's generation has a common mindset that their life is supposed to be better than it was for their parents' generation, and that their children's lives will prosper even more. Since time marches in a straight line, those people living in the present are closer to achieving the "American Dream" than those people that lived on the older parts of the timeline.

This mindset is not unique to today's youth. As a child in the 1950s, I had it better than my parents' generation. My future was the one George Jetson lived in. Disney said so. Whenever there were bumps on the timeline, a new generation just took charge and got America back on the straight and narrow path to prosperity. Whenever hiccups happen, just reboot and move on down the line. This is America, after all.

I believe otherwise now. History is not a directionless bowl of cornflakes, and there is no guarantee that each generation's seat at the table automatically assures them of a better meal. History is more like the slinky I played with as a kid, a circular piece of continuous wire that repeats itself as it goes round and round and up and down.

Slinky

I concur with the works of William Strauss, Neil Howe, and Roy H. Williams that point to different generations of people moving history in cyclical patterns, becoming different about every forty years. History has a rhythm to it, like the seasons of the year. The ethos

Americans are experiencing today is similar to what Americans felt in 1931, 1850, and 1770. The values we hold dear today are not the same values we held dear just 20 years ago. However, they are the same values that were closest to our hearts in the 1940s and at the turn of the 20th century.

Cycles of history

There have been four recurring historical cycles over the past 500 years. They come and go like clockwork. The cycle we are in now has happened before and will occur again. Each cycle lasts about a lifetime.

The easiest cycle to understand is the crisis cycle, one in which our world is turned upside down. The Great Depression and World War II was the last crisis. About one lifetime before that was the Civil War, and a lifetime before that was the American Revolution. This crisis pattern can be followed to Western Europe. If this cycle were a season, it would be winter.

Since winter is always followed by spring, following the crisis cycle are the "good time" years. The crisis is cleaned up, things calm down, and life is wonderful.

Unfortunately, the good times never last too long. The third cycle becomes the summer of discontent. The youth rise up and challenge their elders. Old norms don't cut it anymore, and new norms are introduced.

This sets the table for fall, the next season. People are upset. The last cycle unravels the world order and everyone is at each other's throat. The result is another crisis, then some more good times, then a spiritual revolt, and the cycle repeats itself again and again.

There are numerous, consistent examples of these cycles in our history. After the Great Depression and World War II crisis, there was an American High in which America believed it could do anything. Life settled down and everyone got together to put the world back together. The same attitudes were prevalent after the Civil War and the American Revolution as well.

The 60s and 70s brought about great social turmoil in this country. From the political assassinations to free love, social values were questioned and turned upside down. The "Roaring Twenties" were about women's suffrage and prohibition. Sectionalism over slavery dominated the decade prior to the Civil War. The differences became so pronounced that only another crisis could resolve it.

Generations

Just as we cannot choose our parents, we also cannot choose the generation we were born in. A generation is a group of people born over the space of a lifetime who share a common location in history. People are a part of a generation whether they like it or not. Generations are born and generations die. There is no escaping this. Within each generation's lifetime individuals will certainly differ in a number of ways, but as a group they share a common persona.

Generations get cool names. Fourteen American generations have been named, like Boomers, Generation X, and Millennials. The youngest generation, born after 2003, has no name as of yet. Conventional wisdom would assume that each new generation is an extension of the previous generation. This is not so. No generation is like the generation before it. The truth is that each generation is the opposite of the previous generation. Each new generation's purpose seems to be to compensate for the excesses and mistakes of the last generation.

At any one moment in time, there are multiple generations in play with each at a different stage in life. Today there are six generations of Americans living, the most ever in our history. Generational study is a huge rabbit hole. The short course is that one of two stereotypes of generations, a "me" generation or a "we" generation, takes control for about forty years and sets the agenda for the other living generations to follow. Neither of these stereotypes is superior to the other. Both have their positive and negative extremes.

For example my generation, the Boomer generation, is a "me" generation. We demand freedom of expression and personal liberty. We believe we are unique individuals who possess unlimited potential. The Progressive generation of the late 1800s had the same mindset as us Boomers. The generation that is now taking control, the Millennial generation, is a "we" generation. They demand conformity for the common good. They team up for a common purpose. They think just like the G.I. generation that saved the world in World War II.

Generations move history

Like my slinky, historical patterns are cyclical. The generation in charge pushes the slinky forward. Once pushed, the slinky starts out like a house on fire and then slowly loses its energy, waiting for the next generational push that is just around the corner.

There is no need for added evidence that historical and generational patterns are real. However, looking at my ancestry through my slinky has helped me better understand Kentucky's out migration, Carter County's rise and fall, ghost townitis, and the attitudes and individual behaviors of myself and my family. It also allows me to peek around the corner and see what's coming.

Let's not get too far ahead of ourselves, however. Let's first take a closer look at The Ghost Towns of 174 and the family that lived in and around them.

Kentucky and the Great Migrations

Appalachian assumptions.

Eastern Kentucky, Carter County, and Olive Hill are part of the Appalachian region. Geographically, the region stretches over 13 states and 406 counties. 54 of those counties, including Carter, are in Kentucky. Arguably, the region is huge, however, culturally, Appalachia typically refers only to the central and southern portions of the range.

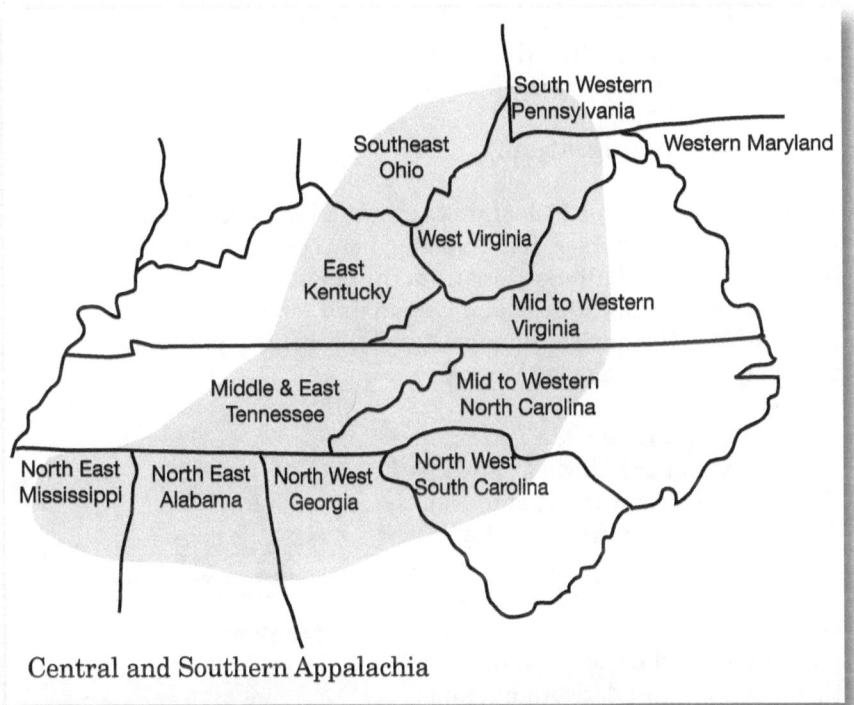

Central and Southern Appalachia

People from this part of Appalachia have often been culturally stereotyped as isolated and old-fashioned when compared to the rest of the people in the United States. They are backward hicks, rednecks, and hillbillies that can't read or talk right, don't use soap or wear shoes. They also beat their kids, friends, neighbors, dogs, are white, racists, and possibly expendable.

Blame Lil Abner and the Beverly Hillbillies for part of this perception, but the ugly truth is that it has been acceptable by many in our society to make fun of this cultural group for a long time. It is not my task to untangle mountain folk prejudices. Stereotypes go both ways and the inside secret is that Appalachian humor from inside the mountain range about outside cultures is just as cruel.

There are thousands of stories buried behind the curtains of Route 174's six ghost towns. If you were able to resurrect and publish them you would find a positive common thread running among them – individualism, self-reliance, pride, family, religion, humor, and patriotism – in good times and bad.

The six thriving little communities didn't become ghost towns without a reason. Understanding that reason starts with understanding Kentucky and the three great migrations.

The first great migration.

Kentucky became the 15th state to join the Union in 1792. It's known for thoroughbred horses, horse racing, bourbon whiskey, bluegrass music, and basketball. Settlers from the colonies had followed Daniel Boone through the Cumberland Gap to find fertile land. Of course they ran into the native Indians who didn't believe in the concept of the 21st century Welcome Wagon.

Manifest Destiny

Manifest Destiny was the notion, not the policy, that the United States had the God given right to expand from the Atlantic to the Pacific. I'm not going to argue the rights or wrongs of Manifest Destiny here, but once Boone found the Gap through the mountains and the pioneers from the Colonies, including those from England, Scotland, and Ireland got a taste of what the West had to offer, the Indian gig was up. President Jackson put the final hammer to that in 1830 with the Indian Removal Act. The Cherokees, the main Appalachian Indian tribe, were removed by the government to the Oklahoma territory.

Under the umbrella of Manifest Destiny, people started moving west and didn't stop until the United States was a bicoastal nation. Kentucky was a portal through which the United States' first great migration entered.

The second great migration.

The second great migration is the focus of this book. It grew out of the Depression and continued after World War II well into the 70s. From the dust bowls of the Midwest people went west, many to California. From the South they went north and joined other northerners who clustered around the industrial cities. Of course many Southerners retained their southern ways and had difficulty adjusting to the North. Many northerners had difficulty accepting the Southerners.

Over 4 million Appalachians left the region due to economic conditions. The Davis family was among the 400,000 plus who left their Kentucky communities for northern cities like Detroit, Pittsburgh, Cleveland, Cincinnati, and Chicago. Our family located in Mansfield, Ohio in 1959, joining other family members who had previously made the move.

Many of the native Kentucky communities never recovered.

Count Kentucky a huge contributor to the country's second great migration.

The third great migration.

The third migration has started. People from the South are returning to their roots as the industrial work in the north has moved south or disappeared off shore. Millions of baby boomers will not spend their retirement years above the Mason-Dixon Line. They are opting for warmer climates and a simpler life down south.

The downside to this third great migration is just starting to be felt. As the people of the South discovered when its people left, money follows people. The loss of people in the North is a loss of revenue and increased pressure to maintain the quality of life and infrastructure for those still there. The gain for the South will be an increase in revenue but a drain on the infrastructure while being forced to provide increased social services and health care.

Kentucky will benefit from this third great migration. Carter County has already experienced a slight population growth. Communities decimated by previous out-migration have learned to function on a reduced tax base and therefore will be attractive to new businesses and those businesses who are tired of higher state and local taxes.

One little recognized aspect of the third migration is the returning of Appalachia's dead sons and daughters. Carter County has over 250 cemeteries and many who transplanted north in the second migration will return to be buried with their families. One of the many Appalachian values is love of place. People from Appalachia never forget "back home." Want proof? Visit any Carter County cemetery on Decoration Day.

We are in the midst of America's third great migration. Kentucky was a gatekeeper in the first and a loser in the second. It could benefit in the third.

Carter County

And then, the fire went out.

From day one, Carter County was a prosperous, blue-collar workhorse county, full of proud, self-reliant, independent piss-and-vinegar patriotic people with strong family values. The county has had various job-related economic activities, ranging from burly tobacco and garment manufacturing to arts and crafts and tourism, but...

...the gold in Carter County has always been its raw materials. The secret behind the county's economic success was the people's ability to find raw material, extract it, make something out of it, and do it all over again once its supply became financially unfeasible and scarce.

For over a hundred years, Carter County's raw materials of iron ore, fire clay, coal, timber, and limestone helped fire the American Industrial Revolution, which, in turn, helped fire the United States' economic growth.

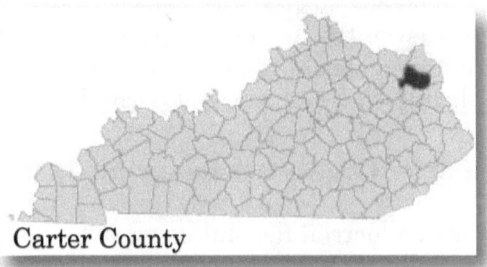

Carter County

Unfortunately, while the county's natural resources were plentiful, they were not unlimited.

Eventually, the fire went out. Carter Countians ran out of new raw materials to prosper from, while the non-mined job-related activities could not carry the county's economic burden. The county's economic activity shriveled up like a burnt piece of paper. Then, as Tom Joad did in Steinbeck's Grapes of Wrath, the county's most valuable asset, its sons and daughters, migrated north with other eastern Kentucky residents to find industrial jobs in Ohio and Michigan.

In comparison to its earlier history, Carter County has fallen on hard times. Outsiders are quick to view Carter County's economic history as an Andy Warhol moment: get its 15 minutes of fame for what its people and natural resources did for its country, then exit stage left for its hard times. Others, on the other hand, see Carter County as a wounded soldier who gave all it had for its country, and is now doing what it can to survive.

County background

Carter County was legislated into existence in 1838, with a population of around 2,300. The land was originally owned by Colonel William Grayson, a prominent Revolutionary War veteran, Virginia delegate to the Constitutional Convention, and US Senator. It was ceded to him by the state of Virginia as a reward for his war services. Carter County is named for the Colonel's grandson, State Senator William Grayson Carter. The county seat, Grayson, is probably named in both their honors.

As of 2010, the county population was 27,462 in a land area of 411 square miles, an average of 69 people per square mile. The county contains a lot of smaller communities like those on Route 174, and just two incorporated cities, Grayson and Olive Hill.

However, the Carter County story is not one of demographics and numbers, but of the rise and fall of its natural resources before, during, and after the Industrial Revolution.

Carter County has footprints in the Industrial Revolution.

The Industrial Revolution wasn't a political, social, or cultural revolution. It was an economic revolution. It started in Great Britain in the late 1700s, spread throughout Europe, and then found a permanent home in America between 1820 and 1870. Carter County has solid footprints in America's Industrial Revolution.

The Industrial Revolution changed the way the world produced its goods. Society went from producing goods by hand in the home, to producing goods by machine in the factory. Carter County's iron ore, coal, timber, fire clay, and limestone industries helped spur the United States in the direction of a modern urban-industrial country.

Iron ore first.

Mark Twain once said, "Everything has its limits. Iron ore cannot be educated into gold." However, iron ore can be used to make steel, and without steel the world would be a flimsy place indeed.

It was the small iron ore furnaces of New Jersey, Pennsylvania, and New England that initially carved out our nation. However, from Andrew Jackson's presidency in 1824 to President Garfield's assassination in 1881, Northeast Kentucky (including Carter County) and Southern Ohio produced most of the iron ore in the United States.

A bonanza of iron ore was discovered in a 100-mile region stretching from Hocking County in Ohio to Carter County in Kentucky. This area came to be called the Hanging Rock Iron Region, and supplied the pioneers with their pots and pans. And, during the Civil War, over 65 furnaces from this region fired out munitions for the boys from Antietam to Appomattox.

The first Kentucky iron ore furnaces showed up in Greenup and Carter Counties around 1825. There were five iron furnaces in Carter County. The oldest was the Pactolus Furnace, built in 1824. Hunnewell Furnace and Boone Furnace, both near the Greenup County line, fired up in 1845 and 1856, respectively. Boone Furnace produced 1,200 to 2,600 tons per year. The Mt. Savage furnace three miles south of Grayson, and Star Furnace near Boyd County, was built in 1848. Mt. Savage turned out about 8.5 tons per day.

Hanging Rock Region

The last blast of these five Carter County iron furnaces occurred in 1885. By the time Theodore Roosevelt spoke softly and carried his big stick in 1901, the once prosperous "Hanging Rock" iron ore industry with its scattered furnaces was no longer financially feasible. It had all disappeared in favor of the big steel city blast furnaces.

Iron Ore memory

And then came fire clay.

Iron ore footprints in the Industrial Revolution were small in comparison to those left by Carter County's fire clay.

Steel making blast furnaces of the Industrial Revolution reached temperatures of 3,000 degrees Fahrenheit. These steel furnaces needed to be lined with something that could withstand this intense heat. The answer to keeping molten steel from burning up a blast furnace was fire bricks made from fire clay, a natural resource not readily found in the 1870s. What was mined was located in small pockets in the east.

By the 1880s, the Industrial Revolution had created a need for more steel, which created the need for more furnaces. More locomotives on more tracks meant more fire boxes. Anything produced with high heat needed fire bricks, which were scarce.

Carter County Firebrick

A man by the name of Charles Taylor had found a little fire clay in Greenup County in the 1860s. He made a few fire bricks in an old brewery in Ashland, hauling the clay from the mines to Ashland by mule-drawn wagons. He then built a second plant in Cincinnati, once he realized it would be easier to float his Greenup County fire clay by barge down the Ohio River, rather than pull the fire clay overland by mules.

And then, Carter County delivered big time. A large deposit of fire clay was discovered in a 400 square mile area around Olive Hill. This clay was near perfect for making the needed bricks, as it had different grades and textures, from gray to white and grainy to more plastic – and there was a lot of it!

Big and small mines began dotting the Carter County landscape. This fire clay discovery in the "Olive Hill District" became a shot-in-the-arm for America's Industrial Revolution, Carter County, and Olive Hill. The timing could not have been better.

Soon, Olive Hill District fire bricks began coating the insides of blast furnaces, kilns, and fireplaces throughout the Midwest, especially in the hotbed steel-making cities of Pittsburgh and Cleveland. Olive Hill fire bricks were used by railroad companies for their locomotive fire boxes, power plants, potteries, coke ovens, and anywhere else high temperatures were encountered. Olive Hill fire bricks were eventually shipped throughout the world.

Brick plant boom.

In the late 1860s, three enterprising gentlemen, Mr. Eifort, Mr. Grahn, and Mr. Staughton, bought 10,000 acres around Olive Hill to build the Tygart Valley Iron Company. They believed the railroad would soon link Ashland and Louisville, piercing the heart of their land purchase and transporting their iron products to market.

Kentucky railroads were now a growing industry. Kentucky had just 78 miles of railroad in 1850, and over 500 miles by 1860. Because the railroad company had just bought the land between Ashland and Louisville, the three opportunity seekers believed that tracks would be laid immediately between the cities. Unfortunately for them, the railroad didn't materialize until 1883, much too late for their Tygart Valley Iron Company to take off.

Karl B. Grahn

The three entrepreneurs then subdivided their 10,000 acres. Grahn took the eastern part, a portion of which is still named for him. Eifort took the central part that housed Olive Hill, and Staughton took the western portion, which included the future ghost towns of Route 174.

Mr. Grahn and Mr. Eifort made nice lemonade out of their lemons. When the railroad was finally constructed, Eifort began shipping the newly discovered Olive Hill fire clay to brick plants in Pennsylvania and Ohio. Mr. Eifort sold his land in 1895, and the first brick plant in Olive Hill was built, aptly named the Olive Hill Fire Brick Company.

Grahn also shipped considerable amounts of fire clay, but he also built a brick plant in Louisville in 1889. Mr. Grahn's Louisville Fire Brick Works later opened up a plant in Grahn, and one in Hitchins in 1913.

In 1900, the Ashland Fire Brick Company erected a brick plant by the Chesapeake and Ohio railroad, on a road that would later become Route 174. Clyde Hayward is credited with the actual building of the plant for the AFBC. The small community that developed around the plant bore his name. The plant averaged 12,000 to 15,000 bricks per day, 3,600 carloads per year. It had seven kilns and was fed its fire clay from a mine just south of the plant.

In 1901, a second brick plant in Olive Hill was built by Harbison-Walker of Pittsburgh. The Kentucky Fire Brick Company built a brick plant in

Haldeman Brick Plant

Haldeman in 1903. The plant at Haldeman was much larger than its Hayward neighbor, producing between 40,000 and 50,000 bricks per day in 14 kilns. Its fire clay was extracted from multiple mines, also close to the plant.

In all, there were about eight fire brick plants built within the Northeast Kentucky fire clay district. Combined, these brick plants produced hundreds of thousands of nine-inch bricks per day. One source calculated this amount of bricks to require 2,000 tons of fire clay, which then filled 50 train carloads of fire bricks.

Unfortunately, from its first diggings, the fire clay industry in Northeast Kentucky was destined to end. That end started materializing in the 1950s, with changes in the steel industry that practically eliminated the need for fire bricks. Oxygen-induction furnaces were invented and quickly became the norm, replacing the need for Olive Hill's fire bricks. Plus, so much of the fire clay had already been mined over the past five decades, that more time would have certainly eventually ended the fire brick run.

Black heat.

Coal was discovered in Kentucky in 1750, and has been mined there ever since. Kentucky is one of the top five coal-producing states in the US, with over 400 coal mines as of 2010. Two major coal fields, Western and Eastern, hide the Kentucky coal. Carter County is among the 30 original Kentucky counties and four adjoining states that comprise the Eastern Mountain Coal Field.

Coal was mined from Carter County in three major intervals. The brickyards needed coal to heat the kilns that made the fire bricks. The miners often mined the fire clay and coal underground at the same time from the same mine. A second boom came during World War II to feed the furnaces that made the ships,

For longer life of industrial coal handling equipment --

Preparation must include

CORROSION PROTECTION

with **PERMATREAT Coal Spray**

The protective action of Permatreat Coal Spray helps prevent breakdown of stoker and other equipment due to corrosion. Unloading trouble, caused by freezing in hopper cars, is reduced; coal is stored and handled easier. Permatreat Coal Spray seals fly-dust to coal, eliminates the dust nuisance.

One of our representatives, highly trained in coal treating, will be glad to give you facts on treating of industrial coals. Write today; no obligation.

Ashland PERMATREAT COAL SPRAY seals in dust

ASHLAND OIL & REFINING COMPANY Ashland, Kentucky

planes, and tanks. A third boom occurred in the 1970s with the advent of strip mining.

Although there are currently more than 20 Kentucky counties mining the Eastern coal field, Carter County is not among them. Better coal that was easier to mine was found elsewhere, falling prices, labor disputes, and increased government regulations all helped end Carter County's coal production. Yet, over 1.7 billion tons of coal was extracted from Carter County from the mid-1800s to 1993.

Carter's other natural resources.

Salt Peter, or sodium nitrate, was mined during the War of 1812 to make gun powder. This resource was found in caves in the northeast part of Carter county. These caves were to later become a major tourist draw and one of the state's best parks and resort areas, Carter Caves State Park.

There was also an abundance of timber and limestone in Carter County. Logging and saw milling was always a prominent industry, beginning with the explosion of the railroad companies. A lot of railroad cross-ties are made with timber from Carter County trees.

And limestone mining hit its high point in the 1920s, as there were ten quarries producing this rock. The most notable quarry for our family was in Lawton, behind the Rayburn store.

A work in progress.

Much of Carter County's history is about extracting material from the earth. From Salt Peter to iron ore, to fire clay, coal, timber, and limestone, Carter County's abundance of natural resources helped create a series of economic booms for its population. But then, the raw material fire went out and cold crept into the county.

Carter County played well the natural resource cards it was dealt in the 19th and early 20th centuries. The game continues today, but the hands coming from the new deck are not as strong. A deeper look into Carter County today will find dedicated leaders, and community- and faith-based groups working hard to enhance the quality of life in Carter County.

The proud history of Carter County is still a work in progress.

US Route 60

"At age 9, I thought all roads led to US Route 60..."

Today, two main highway arteries lazily wind their way east and west through Carter County: US Route 60 and Interstate 64. While the two roads intertwine three times, they only have one point of direct access.

Of course, I-64 is a part of the National Highway System and a Johnny-Come-Lately when it comes from getting from here to there. Drones could drive on I-64, like on most other interstate highways. Wide-open and boring, I-64 was non-existent in my youth.

From the backseat of our 54 Ford, however, US Route 60 seemed to be the highway of all highways.

US Route 60 today is a 2,760 mile, two-lane road running from Virginia to Arizona. A large eastern portion of Rt. 60 is the old Midland Trail, one of the oldest east-west routes in America.

The Midland Trail began in Virginia and eventually stretched westward. The trail was initially carved out by animals, surveyed by a young George Washington, and traveled over by Indians, pioneers, stage coaches and Civil War soldiers. Settlements like Grayson and Olive Hill birthed. Mom-and pop businesses opened to serve those traveling on the trail. When the state highway system took over in the early 1920s, the Midland Trail was given a number – US Route 60.

Salt

What possessed those animals to carve out a path in the first place has everything to do with why Kentucky beat Ohio and Tennessee to statehood. The answer is salt.

A little-known fact is that population shifts and even the rise and fall of civilizations are directly proportional to the availability of salt. No salt, no civilization. No salt at the end of the rainbow? No pot of gold to be found.

Salt is an essential part of our diet and is vital to our survival. Early pioneers itching to settle into the Ohio and Kentucky territories needed a gun, an axe, a good horse, a good wife, and lots of good luck. They also needed salt for consumption and the preservation of their meat.

Before the Declaration of Independence, salt was brought into the colonies from the West Indies. Lugging this salt westward in the early innings of Manifest Destiny was burdensome and expensive for pioneers. It would be necessary for the pioneers to have salt available once they arrived in the west.

Done.

Salt licks are prevalent in Kentucky. Boone and a bunch of axmen cut a 200-mile path called The Wilderness Road through the mountains, which were a natural barrier for east-to-west pioneer travel. At the end of the Road, Boone built Kentucky's first settlement at Boonesborough. It was from Boonesborough that later pioneers spread out in all directions to settle new territories.

Boone chose the location for Boonesborough because of its proximity to the Kentucky River and closeness to a salt spring. Daniel Boone knew how to make temporary furnaces, remove the water, dry the remaining salt slush, and produce ¼ pound of salt from each gallon of water. He taught other pioneers how to make salt and how to locate salt springs.

Armed with this knowledge, pioneers traveled north from Boonesborough and headed south either to the Tennessee territory, further west, or north towards Ohio.

Some of the early Boonesborough pioneers who pushed the geographic envelope settled in and around future Carter County where they found salt springs.

The ancestors of today's highways can be traced back to these salt springs. Like spokes on a wagon wheel, wild animals and people from nearby settlements created paths to the salt springs. These paths first became footpaths, then wagon trails, then stagecoach routes, then automobile roads, and now national highways.

In essence, Olive Hill, Morehead, and Route 60 that connects them are where they are today because of salt.

Bookend cities.

Route 60 may have been over 2,000 miles long, but as a youth I really only traveled about 80 miles of it. Our daily world existed on State Route 174, an 11-mile stretch of two-lane road that started and stopped on Route 60.

The distance between Olive Hill and Morehead is only about 20 miles on Route 60, but I never traveled those 20 miles. We always traveled TO Olive Hill or TO Morehead – never from one book end city to the other.

I only remember traveling west of Morehead on Route 60 once or twice, to Mt. Sterling. As far as I was concerned, west of Morehead was the end of the earth. However, we did travel east on Route 60 a lot: it was about 60 miles to Ashland to see Aunt Julia and Uncle Earl, Mom's favorite aunt and my namesake.

US Route 60, through our two book-end cities of Olive Hill and Morehead, was our portal to the rest of the Universe. But Route 174, its communities, and its people, was where our daily life unfolded.

Olive Hill

"It was the best of times, it was the worst of times..."

...were the first words from Dickens' classic novel A Tale of Two Cities. They describe well the ups and downs of Olive Hill. Although the latest census figures indicate that there is a slight population growth in Carter County, the Olive Hill population continues to decline. It wasn't always that way.

Here are two Carter County news clippings that will give you a positive glimpse of Olive Hill life in the early 1900s during the brick plant boom:

Olive Hill in the late 50s

May 23, 1900
OLIVE HILL   Dr. John L. Robins a resident of the Olive Hill has a home known as the Castle. He lives on a point overlooking the town and has a winter house containing 9 rooms, all of which are furnished, also a summer house within twenty feet of the winter house with ten rooms also furnished, so the moving from one house to the other is but small task as there is no furniture to be moved.

July 14, 1909
OLIVE HILL   We spent Thursday night at Olive Hill. The town is booming. Both fire clay plants are in full force day and night. The population is fully 3,000. Much improvement has been made during the past year. In April the third bank for the town began business. Olive Hill is no slouch. It is a hustling growing town that is coming to the front with large modern business houses well lighted and with concrete pavements. The town is alive and it does not depend for revenue upon saloon licenses. Its people are sensible and have learned a lesson. Its drunks are imported from other towns.

Olive Hill's roots can be traced back to the early 1830s as a trading post. It was a stagecoach stop along current highway U.S. 60 which eventually connected Washington D.C. and Los Angeles. Olive Hill was originally located on a hill overlooking Tygarts Creek, named after Michael Tygart, an early Kentucky explorer.

As the story goes, Olive Hill was named by Elias P. Davis (no relation) for his friend Thomas Oliver, the oldest resident in the area. Davis named the village Oliver Hill. And, as the story continues, the name was just too hard to roll off the tongue easily, so villagers just shortened it to Olive Hill.

Plus, to confuse matters even more, the upcoming railroad had not planned to chug its way up that hill to get to the little town without an "r" in its name. So, the town's folk decided to move from the "hill" to the "valley" and relocate near the scenic Tygarts Creek and by the new railroad tracks.

So, Olive Hill is not really on a hill, and its name is really missing an "r" because, like the Holland bridge in World War II, it was a syllable too far. Of course, Oliver Hill, a famous Civil Rights attorney of the 50s and 60s, had no trouble with that extra "r" in his name. Neither did Oliver Hill, the famous English architect.

Early 1900s Railroad Street

Olive Hill was incorporated into a city in 1884, and, for a couple of months became the county seat of newly formed Beckham County in 1904. However, the Court ruled that Beckham County did not meet the population requirements and ordered it dissolved. That was the only county in the state that has ever been abolished.

In addition to judicial abandonment, Olive Hill has had its share of natural disasters. An overflowing Tygarts Creek has flooded Olive Hill numerous times, while major fires have also economically impacted the downtown area.

February 1, 1936
OLIVE HILL Four brick structures, including the 30-room Stamper hotel, were gutted by flames and damages estimated at $100,000 were caused here Friday by a fire that burned for more than two hours before it was brought under control. In addition to the hotel the blaze destroyed Scott's barber shop, the Farmers' hardware store, the Modern Plumbing Heating Co. and the Grizzel five and-10-cent store. Sloan's jewelry store and the U. S. post office building were threatened with destruction for a time and water damage was said to be high in the jewelry store.

Olive Hill also has some Civil War history. Kentucky was a border state, and like people in other border states, Carter County and Olive Hill residents had split allegiances. There were slave-owning families and approximately 300 slaves in Carter County when the war erupted.

Early in the war, Confederate General John Hunt Morgan and his "Raiders" harassed northern General George Morgan's Union force of 8,000 men close to Olive Hill. It seems that northern Morgan was moving his troops from Cumberland Gap to Ohio, while southern Morgan was in the area just looking for some trouble. It was a dust up, not a battle.

Kentucky has produced a lot of notable people. Carter County has produced its fair share of entertainers, authors, artists, and politicians. Three people stand out originating from Olive Hill: Tom T. Hall, William Jason Fields, and Matthew Sellars.

Matthew Sellers

Tom T. is a country music singer and songwriter who has penned 11 #1 hit songs. Born in Olive Hill in 1936, Hall has written songs recorded by Johnny Cash, George Jones, Loretta Lynn, Waylon Jennings, Alan Jackson, and Bobby Bare.

"Wild Bill from Olive Hill" Fields was a prominent Kentucky Governor from 1923 to 1927.

Matthew Sellars was an inventor who conducted early aeronautical research and made the first powered airplane flight in Kentucky in 1908. Matthew invented and patented the retractable landing gear. He left the Grahn area shortly after 1911, and was later hailed as one of America's great flying men along with Orville and Wilbur Wright.

A Saturday town.

Olive Hill had a reputation for being a Saturday town, with rural folks from surrounding communities, like us, heading there to spend their day off. As a kid, I never saw the seedy Saturday night side of Olive Hill life. As an adult with 14 years of experience in the criminal justice field, I now find the criminal side of the Olive Hill area interesting. A few news clippings around the turn of the 20th century demonstrate that law enforcement was sparse, while vigilantism was a normal part of life.

May 16, 1881
The Regulators of Carter County have effected a thorough organization for the summer campaign, and will ride in full force during the entire season, punishing with merciless justice all evildoers. Last Thursday night on the Smoky fork of the Buffalo Fork of Tygart, a party of vigilantes visited the house of Townsend Bellamy. He was accused of incest. He and his three sons and son-in-law were whipped three or four weeks ago for gross immorality. This time the Regulators intended to hang the unnatural father. They surrounded the house and attempted to force an entrance. Bellamy made his escape from the house by a rear door and made a bold break for liberty. The Regulators fired upon him, and he fell with five balls in his body. He is not expected to live.

May 19, 1892
OLIVE HILL   There will be called for trial this criminal court a murder case almost without a parallel. On Aug 13 1890 Richard Kizer of this county walked over to his neighbor Henry James and shot him to death in the presence of his family. There was no provocation save a dispute over some cattle a few days previous. Kizer has walked freely around ever since under a small bond.

February 23, 1899
ENTERPRISE An officer armed with a warrant for the arrest of

Harry and Gallon Sloan, Limestone, accused of stealing tobacco from Widow Hide and robbing W.L. Gearheart & Company. On entering the house Harry commenced cutting the officer with a knife. Deputy Tom Rice shot Harry four times, killing him instantly. He shot Gallon through the breast and he is now thought to be dying.

December 4, 1907
OLIVE HILL In a free-for-all fight at a distillery near Olive Hill, Frank Hall was shot and killed and Charlie Garvin was stabbed nine times and is not expected to live.

July 21, 1908
OLIVE HILL Elmer James, aged 19 years, living six miles north of here, was found dead in the road today. He left his wife and baby early in the morning to work his crop. Before noon a passing neighbor found him with a gunshot wound through the back. There is no clue.

What was Olive Hill's focal point?

Of course, one's first mental image of Olive Hill depended on when one lived in the area. Residents near the end of the 19th century would say that the train depot was the focal point of the city. There is no question that the railroad and all its depots were the spark for the area's population and economic growth for many years.

In Olive Hill's heyday, the Chesapeake and Ohio passed seven trains a day through Olive Hill, with additional stops at small depots east and west of Olive Hill. President Truman even made a "whistle-stop" campaign appearance in Olive Hill before defeating Dewey in 1948.

Olive Hill residents of the first few decades of the 20th

Olive Hill Brickies

century would claim the heart of the city to be the two Olive Hill brick plants. In 1942, the two plants employed 1,700 people, almost the whole population of Olive Hill today. They fired out a lot of bricks that made steel for our World War II effort.

In the 1920s the plants sponsored the traveling amateur baseball "Brickies." In 1938 and 1940 the Olive Hill Merchants, another local team, went 42-2.

Olive Hill High School

Teenagers in the 1950s might see the city's focal point as either the long standing James Drive-In or the local roller skating rink, popular cultural hang-outs of the times.

To me, looking back on my childhood, the city's focal point was the Olive Hill High School.

Originally built in 1929 and subsequently closed in the 1970s as a high school, this three-story brick building sat high on the north hill overlooking downtown Olive Hill. The original Olive(r) Hill village was located on a hill south of Tygarts Creek. From Route 60, Olive Hill's Main Street, there were 103 stone steps leading up to the then humongous school, all built by a local WPA chapter.

I have never actually been in the school building, but I did march in a parade in front of it. Plus, the baseball field where Harlan and I played Little League ball was behind it.

As a kid attending elementary school in the county, I saw the high school building on the hill as a real, not perceived, symbol of higher education. Mom had made it clear that both my brother and I would pass through that school on our way to a good college education.

After closing down, the school building went into considerable disrepair, but through the efforts of local people it was saved from demolition and has now been partially renovated. It currently houses the Olive Hill Historical Society and holds many cultural community events.

Here is my favorite Olive Hill High School news clipping, written just before I was born:

Feb 4, 1947
Most anything can happen in a basketball game. The other night at Olive Hill, Jack Jaynes star guard of the team, was called to the telephone during a time out. When he returned smiling all over he yelled, "it's a boy and weighs 8 pounds". Jaynes is a senior on the Comet quintet. His wife is the former Miss Betty Bocook and she attended school with her husband.

Olive Hill holds a lot of my firsts.

As a family, we always went to Olive Hill to do something, to get something accomplished, never just to hang out. Upon our return home from Olive Hill, some task was always completed. Whether grocery shopping, a baseball game, a hamburger, or a haircut, it was in Olive Hill that I experienced a lot of my firsts.

My first haircut was at Stephen's Barber Shop on Railroad Street, across from the old Stamper Hotel. I quickly learned what I liked and didn't like about the hair cutting experience. Only at Stephens could I get my hair cut where it tapered or blended in the back. At any other place my Dad took me, I would wind up with a "bowl on the head haircut" like Moe from The Three Stooges. I wore a lot of hats as a youth, primarily to cover the back of my head.

Harlan and I first played baseball at Olive Hill. There were six Little League teams and we were on the Cards, with blue and white uniforms. As the coach handed us our uniforms right before the first game, Harlan and I changed into them in the car. We both remember this moment well because we didn't know how to put on our stirrup socks. How were we to know that the socks went over another pair of socks, and the small stirrup slid under the heel? We actually thought the stirrup went

Cards stars

between the big toe and its neighbor toe, and it took us a while to figure it out.

Harlan and I saw our first professional baseball game sometime around 1957 as a result of our Little League participation. Bussed from Olive Hill to Crosley Field in Cincinnati, we Little Leaguers watched the Reds double play combo of McMillan to Temple to no shirt sleeves Klusezwski. I had never seen such an immaculate playing field as Crosley.

Olive Hill was my first movie, around the early 1950s. King Kong. Fay Wray. The movie was made in 1933 and I will never know why it took so long to run at the Dixie Theater in downtown Olive Hill.

I attended my first carnival just west of Olive Hill on Route 60, between the brick plant and downtown. I remember seeing the Ferris Wheel from a distance, but I do not remember riding it, or any other rides for that matter. I also didn't understand why women were standing by their tents, tantalizing men to come inside. However, I did want to see the Wild Man from some far away land who could scratch his armpits.

Other firsts.

- I saw my first traffic light in Olive Hill, its the only one on Railroad Street. It had no cautionary yellow, just green and red.
- I marched in my first parade on Main Street.
- I attended my first funeral in Henderson's funeral home. The Henderson family and burials can be traced back to 1825. Until then, I had only attended wakes in homes where the deceased had lived.
- I visited my first bus station and saw my first Greyhound bus.
- I remember eating in a restaurant in Olive Hill. The restaurant was part of the Stamper Hotel.
- I first roller skated in Olive Hill. I remember Aunt Patty, in her poodle skirt and white skates, and thought she was pretty. I fell a lot on my skates.
- I saw my first Doctor in Olive Hill, Doc Fortune. He delivered me, although I don't remember that incident. Duh! All future doctor visits were in Morehead or to the Kings Daughters hospital in Ashland, where I got my tonsils removed and ate a lot of ice cream.

Unfortunately, Olive Hill is experiencing some of its worst times. However, for a kid growing up, Olive Hill provided me some of my best times.

Brickie Ball Park, 1925

Olive Hill Brick Plant

Hitchens Brickyard 1920's

Morehead

The college town of Morehead was a smart place...

...in fact, it was the smartest city I knew, since that's where
Morehead State College was located. As a youth, I imagined the name
Morehead came from putting together two words, more and head.
Apparently, this is not so. The town is actually named for a Kentucky
former governor, James T. Morehead. Shucks.

Morehead is the county seat of Rowan County, also named for a
former Kentucky politician. Kentucky statehooded during
Washington's presidency and Rowan County and Morehead came into
being just before Lincoln's time. Whatever happened there between
Washington and Lincoln's presidencies was insignificant to what
happened afterwards.

Ground zero.

From 1884 to the summer of 1887, Morehead was ground zero for the
Rowan County War. Over 20 people were killed and another 16
wounded during the Martin-Tolliver-Logan family feud.

The seeds of Morehead's
Rowan County War can
be traced back to the
Civil War. Although
Kentucky remained
neutral in the Civil War,
nevertheless, North and
South loyalties split
many families and
divided lawyers, judges
and politicians. In the
years following the Civil
War, hatred between the
two sides festered and

built up to where they were killing each other like flies at a picnic.
Abolishing the second amendment was never discussed.

The final clash of this death dance occurred in June of 1887. The
Tollivers had usurped a political and law enforcement stranglehold on

Morehead. They had pissed off a lot of people, including Daniel Boone Logan. Many Rowan County residents had left for greener pastures, but D.B. stayed and recruited a vigilante army. They surrounded the Tolliver family in Morehead's Central Hotel with the ultimatum "Get out or die." The Tollivers chose to die, which they did grudgingly in a two-hour 1,500 plus bullet western style shoot-out.

As a child I never knew anything about these families or their disagreements.

Birthplace of adult education.

Cora Wilson Stewart (1875-1958) was an elementary school teacher and county school superintendent in eastern Kentucky's Rowan County. In the fall of 1911 she opened 50 school classrooms to adult pupils. More than 1,200 men and women from 18 to 86 attended opening night.

Stewart later wrote, *"Among them were not alone illiterate farmers and their illiterate wives, sons, and daughters, but also illiterate merchants or storekeepers, illiterate ministers, and illiterate lumbermen. Mothers, bent with age, came that they might learn to read letters from absent sons and daughters, and that they might learn for the first time to write them."*

The classes were held at night and called "moonlight schools" as the moon casted enough light for students to see the footpaths and wagon trails they had to follow to reach the school. It was estimated that in about four years 40,000 Kentucky adults had learned to read and write in moonlight schools. Cora Stewart? You go girl!

Charlie.

Another one of Morehead's claims to fame is the fact that Charles Manson spent some time there. He was born in Cincinnati during the Great Depression to an alcoholic mother who, as the story goes, sold Charles for a pitcher of beer to a childless waitress.

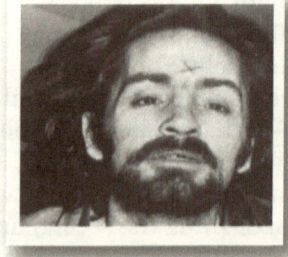

Charles' mother was raised near Olive Hill in Grahn. As Charles recounted himself in a 1980s San Quentin interview, Charles spent some time in Morehead before heading out to the West Coast and forming the infamous Manson Family.

Dad, can you turn up the volume?

We lived about ten miles from the town of Morehead. From our house, we would take Route 174 West to Route 60, take a soft left and ten minutes later we would be pulling into Morehead. About four miles out of Morehead, there was a straight-away that you could safely pass another car. It was always a real bummer for Harlan and I when an oncoming car blocked Mom or Dad from "flooring" it to get around another car.

Harlan and I knew every inch of the drive to Morehead. For me, Morehead started about two miles from downtown, at the Skyline drive-in. The entrance to the drive-in was at the corner of Route 32 and 60. I remember that because Route 32 is half of Route 60. Well, almost.

Skyline Drive-in

Now that I think back to it, we never traveled down Route 32 past the drive-in entrance, even though Sandy Hook was down that road. Seemed like we always knew someone who knew someone who lived or traveled to Sandy Hook.

The drive-in's large screen was turned at an angle, so cars traveling west toward Morehead couldn't see the picture. On the way back home, however, we always waited for that one moment of excitement when we would catch a glimpse of the movie for a few fleeting seconds.

America loved its cars and the drive-in was the perfect place for Davis family outings. It was there at the Skyline that I met John Wayne, Lester Flatt and Earl Scruggs. John, of course, stayed on film, but Lester, Earl and the Foggy Mountain Boys bluegrassed one Saturday night on top of the concession stand between shows. I guess they played wherever they could play when they were still unknowns.

Mom baked with Martha White flour, which soon became Lester and Earl's endorsed product.

At the drive-in, Dad always stayed behind the wheel. Harlan and I stayed in the backseat. In fact, I never made the front seat until I had my own car. I still don't know how we managed to watch Glen Ford's Blackboard Jungle over the front seat, between Dad's right shoulder, Mom's left shoulder and the rearview mirror. In the end, despite the blocked view, we did manage to have a good time going to the drive-in as a family. So many years later, I can still hear that intermission jingle rolling around in my phonological loop and can see the hot dog jumping into the naked bun.

As we watch movies today in our "home theatres" with surround sound I often think about a family of four sitting in a car watching a two hour movie with the sound coming from a three inch speaker hanging on the driver's side window.

Creek swimming.

Just up the road from the drive-in hung two acres of tobacco in a silver-tin, square-shaped, windowless warehouse. It took about ten seconds to drive past the long, one-story building. I never saw any cars around this warehouse, nor activity of any kind, nor any tobacco. I was told the warehouse "hung" tobacco, but always wondered what else might be hung there.

We discovered a creek behind this warehouse. Once, our family went picnicking and swimming with Aunt Marge, Uncle Herman, Woody, Sybil and James in the creek. The big bend in the creek meant there was deep water. We must not have been the first ones to discover this place, since shadowing this bend was a large tree with a hanging rope. I remember Uncle Herman swinging out on that rope and dropping down, but no one else followed suit.

MSU.

Morehead is home to Morehead

Go Eagles

State University, formerly Morehead State Normal School and Teachers College, Morehead State Teachers College and Morehead State College. The school was founded in 1887, the same year Punxsutawney Phil first saw his shadow in Pennsylvania, about six years after the Earps did in the rustlers at the O.K. Corral, and the end of the Tollivers in the Rowan County War.

The only famous people I know of that graduated from MSU is Phil Simms, former quarterback for the NFL New York Giants and MVP of Super Bowl XXI, and Billy Ray Cyrus, Achy-Breaky Heart singer and Miley Cyrus' dad. I also think one or two Miss Kentucky winners graduated as an Eagle.

Plus, Mom graduated from Morehead. It only took her 17 years.

"I had finished high school in three years and entered Morehead at the age of fifteen. No student has enough money to eat and I went hungry many times. The lunch tickets were sold by books and cost five dollars each. I was forever writing home or getting a message through Mr. Bailey's telephone to Dad for money. At one time I hocked a ring for $5, and I know that Esther went into the cash drawer at the store and sent me money without Dad knowing."

Mom was teaching at Soldier when she graduated.

"I finally finished college and received my degree in 1958. I had started in 1941 before the war. In walking across the platform to receive the degree, Harlan was plainly heard saying, "That is my Mom."

The MSU campus was located off Route 60, on a snake-like side street that began before downtown Morehead and ended back on Route 60 in the center of downtown, near the Courthouse.

All the campus buildings were located on the right side of the street, as I recall. The first building was a square brick building that I never entered, Baird Music Hall. Next to the Music Hall was Breckenridge Hall, the "prison" that held Harlan and I during the summer after my third grade.

No, we weren't behind in our schoolwork. Heavens, Harlan had just begun to read and I was doing just fine. Summer school was just another way for Mom to remind us of the high educational bar she had set for us. We knew we were going to college before we were potty trained. It was at Breckenridge Hall that summer that I spread-eagled my first and only butterfly collection. I accidentally tore the wings off a black and yellow Monarch while trying to flatten it out between the cotton and glass. The poor thing didn't stand a chance.

The university built a field house on Route 60, just before the entrance to the campus – it was the largest building I had ever been in. It seated a whopping 5,000 people. Mom and Dad took us there to see Meadow Lark Lemon squash the Washington Generals, as they always did.

We also saw Jerry Lee Lewis perform there. Jerry literally tore up his piano at the end of the show and I was lucky enough to catch one of the keys. The next morning at church, I gave it to Sharon Clevenger as a token of my love. I was crushed when she didn't get the significance of my one gesture.

When we went to see the Morehead College theatrical department's production of The Wizard of Oz, I cowered as the cowardly lion went into the audience and shook my hand.

While Mom was a student, we went swimming in the college Natatorium, where all the women wore swimming caps. Mom was the one in the white cap. No wait, every woman's cap was white.

Go to Town.

For our family, Morehead was a place we went to get things done. Doctors' appointments, car shopping, grocery shopping, movie nights at the drive-in, most of our common family functions centered on Morehead.

Dr. Blair's office was on Main Street, close to the courthouse. When I fell off the school swing set and broke my wrist, he set it in place. I don't remember him taking any X-rays. Dr. Blair was also the one who gave me shots for my poison ivy. It took lots of Calamine lotion and a three-injection shot series to save me after multiple poison ivy breakouts.

The Fannin Ford dealership was just down the street from Dr. Blair's office. Back then, everyone seemed to drive either a Ford or a Chevy. Dad was the one who did the buying. I never went to the dealership with him. I don't think Mom was too pleased with Dad's solo decision-making when he surprised her by bringing home a brand new 1949 Ford one day. Somehow I remember that.

My orthodontist's office was also in Morehead, on Main Street. The braces consisted of a strand of chicken wire attached to a flesh-colored palate that was customized to the roof of my mouth.

I learned how to loosen this torture device by slipping my tongue on the back of the palate and pressing forward. This allowed me the pleasure of rolling the monstrosity around in my mouth like a hot-ball piece of atomic candy. My teeth did eventually straighten out, but I think it had more to do with Clyde Fultz's fist in the second grade.

Ray's grocery store was another one of our family's stops in Morehead. Every Friday, we went grocery shopping as a family. Small by today's standards, Ray's was Mom's favorite. We didn't go out to eat before or after grocery shopping; in fact, we rarely did. Instead, we did our grocery shopping and then Mom fixed dinner at home.

Our regular Friday night treat in the late 1950s was heat-and-serve apple dumplings. Some food manufacturer struck a gold mine with our family, as we must have consumed thousands of four-pack apple dumplings wrapped in bright-silver tin foil. I always wondered how that company could possibly know that we were a family of four. To this day, that Friday night ritual is vivid in my mind every time I eat an apple dumpling.

Beyond going to the drive-in, we found other entertainment options in Morehead. On a few occasions, we went to the Trail movie theatre, where watching "Old Yeller" die was as traumatic for me as learning the truth about Santa Clause.

One summer in my youth, I was a member of the Olive Hill little league all-star team. We played against an all-star team from Winchester on the little league field in Morehead. It was probably my first away athletic game. My team's dream of making it to the finals in Williamsport, wherever that was, was crushed by a score of 30-1. That game gave me my first experience playing against a black athlete. He was a tough pitcher; at one point, he called a time out and pulled a tooth from his mouth while on the mound. I wonder how we even managed to score one run during that game.

Later on in life, Morehead became home to my aunt and my grandmother. Harlan attended MSU for two years before transferring to Bowling Green. As the years went on, Morehead became the city where the funerals for my mom, grandfather and aunts were held.

For a Carter County boy of twelve, Rowan County Morehead was the smartest city I knew.

The Ghost Towns of 174

State Route 174 begins and ends on US Route 60.

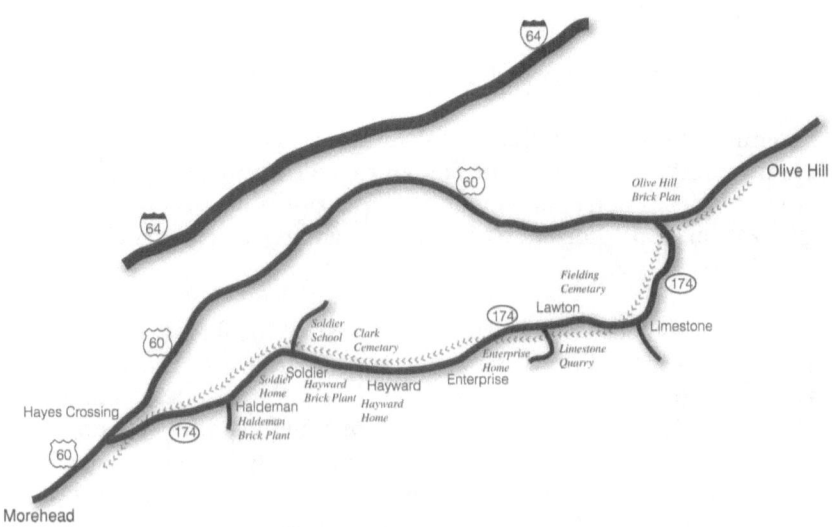

All in all, State Route 174 is just a little over 11 miles long. It weaves along Tygart's Creek and around and through the rolling hills south of Route 60. There are only a few safe spots straight enough for the adventuresome to pass other cars.

Certainly there were early pioneers along this stretch of ground before the 1880s. And certainly there was a roughed-out trail that got them, their horses and wagons to and from town for trade.

The Chesapeake and Ohio railroad connecting Ashland and Louisville was routed through Olive Hill and through the future communities of Hayward and Haldeman in 1883. The search for fire clay in the "Olive Hill District" a few years later uncovered numerous clay mines along the railroad's path. There was now a profit motive to build two brick plants near the railroad, which happened in 1900 in Hayward and in 1903 in Haldeman.

People needed accessibility to and from those plants, and the bricks those people produced needed to be shipped to the rest of the world. The once-sparse people trail and brand-new railroad soon became a decades-old parallel partnership that eventually linked six active social communities. The railroad has since been removed, leaving the road to carry what transportation burden is left from those communities.

The Communities.

Haldeman. Soldier. Hayward. Enterprise. Lawton. Limestone.

As a child, I knew these places as communities of people who lived in close proximity to a school, church, store, train stop, or work. They were not cities. I don't remember mayors, councils, or social organizations, but there must have been some political structures somewhere.

I don't know which community evolved first or the fastest or why, but I do know how one of them got their name – Hayward. If there was any bad blood among the communities, it was well hidden from us children. Each community was unique, but tied together like an Underground Railroad. It was a geographic bucket brigade as each community passed its passer-bys safely to the next one. It was like the school game Red Rover Red Rover, send the people on over.

As an adult, I'm constantly asking how things get done and why. But, as a child, I had no concern for logistics, never questioning where the mines were, how the fire clay got to the kilns, or how 60,000 finished firebricks a day got to the railroad for shipment. Preacher worked at the Sand Plant at some point, but how was sand associated with the fire clay or limestone industries?

Mom, Dad, Preacher, Esther, and all our Aunts and Uncles have shared stories with Harlan and me – personal stories about their lives and their memories on Route 174. I invite you to join Harlan and me in the back seat of our family Ford, circa mid-50s. Gaze with us out the back side windows as we pass through the future Ghost Towns of 174.

As we begin our journey, Morehead is in our rear view mirror.

HALDEMAN

It's just a gentle right turn onto State Route 174 from Route 60 at Hayes Crossing. Up the hill, over the unguarded tracks, around a few curves, and about a mile down the road is Haldeman, a community probably named after someone associated with brick making.

Haldeman is the only one of our Route 174 communities not in Carter County. Everything about Haldeman is Rowan County. And, most everything in Haldeman is on the right side of our car because the railroad tracks run the entire left side. Every community has a general store, and Haldeman is no exception. The Haldeman store is on our right, next to the storeowner's house, the nicest house in Haldeman. I have noticed that the nicest house always belongs to the local storekeeper. The other Haldeman houses, if any, are always invisible to me from the road.

Further down from the store, on the right once again, is the baseball field. Sitting in our car, it's as if we are sitting in the cheap seats in the far right field. Once, dad took us there to watch a Soldier-Haldeman baseball game. No uniforms; in fact, the players wore jeans and t-shirts and shared baseball gloves.

"Cooge was very athletic in his young days. Everett Carpenter told me one time about him playing baseball. I asked him about this, and he said that there was a team from Olive Hill that played. He played first base for them when he wanted to – that was the problem, no commitment. He knew every player on every league and even knew their positions and batting averages. After the boys were older and also knew, they would sit at the table and quiz me. The three of them would make fun of their mother."

Down a bit from the field, still on the right, is the Haldeman school, part of Rowan County's education system. Dad takes us over there sometimes and hits us grounders and fly balls on the school's back lot. There is not much else about this school that is important to me. After just a few seconds, we have passed the school and are looking at the most noticeable structures in Haldeman, the brickyard kilns.

The Haldeman brick plant has fired out an average of 50,000 firebricks per day for years, a much larger output than the Hayward plant down the road. Fourteen kilns harden the bricks, and about half of them are visible from the road.

Past the kilns are the company offices, the local church, and a steep hill that takes us up and away from Haldeman and down and around to Soldier. While just two miles away geographically, psychologically it seems more like 1,000 miles away.

SOLDIER

Soldier and Haldeman are just a high school cross country meet apart. Both communities lie on flat ground with a big hill separating them, the biggest hill the 11-mile stretch of Route 174 crosses.

At the top of the hill is the Rowan and Carter County line. About a mile down the backside of the hill is "downtown" Soldier, with our house being about halfway down that incline. It's the third home our family has lived in on Route 174.

"After renting from the brick plant and Dad in Enterprise we bought our first house in Soldier. The house was formerly owned by a bootlegger. I did not know this, and we had several calls at the back door after dark. Cooge thought this was funny and enjoyed answering the door. There was a lot of remodeling to be done – a new pump in the cellar, furnace, bathroom remodeled, and carpet on the floors. We thought we had died and gone to heaven."

This house is in another world compared to our previous two houses. For the first time, the bathroom is inside. Two people at once can stand on the furnace grate for heat. It has a

Our Soldier Home

garage out by the road, but it's more of a lean-to than a garage as it leans toward "downtown" Soldier. There's a separate "smokehouse" that we use as an extra bedroom, an outdoor cellar that feels like a darkened mausoleum but keeps things cool, and a small rectangular barn in the back of the house that stays empty.

Harlan and I play together a lot here. We play two-man baseball with a set of rules that would make the IRS proud. Once we took off early one morning with our BB guns to hunt dinner and killed a robin, which pretty much destroyed our desire to hunt anything anymore.

We ride our bicycles a lot, including the glide down the road to Mabel and Thurman's general store. But it is a bear peddling back up that road with milk, bread, sugar, and ugh, five pounds of Martha White flour.

Mom occasionally takes us for long walks behind the house. There are numerous dirt roads back there where Mom says the bootleggers quietly kept their goods away from the revenuers.

"Cooge lost his job at the brick plant and started work in Mansfield. The boys and I stayed the summer while I sold the house and packed for our move to Mansfield. He was afraid for me to stay alone, so on one trip home he brought me a gun. I slept with it under my pillow. From the time the boys were small I would hear their prayers at night. The last sentence was always 'and don't let me get old.' But when they found that gun that summer, they added another line to the prayer, 'and don't let Mom shoot someone.'"

The train tracks from Haldeman to Soldier go around the hill. Therefore, the tracks are hidden from view until they reappear and run right through Soldier's gut. There's also a creek that shows its watery head in Soldier and runs through Hayward, Enterprise, and Lawton, joining Tygart's Creek just below Limestone. The creek doesn't have a name and I don't know where it originates.

Unlike Haldeman's invisible housing, Soldier houses are visibly scattered like granite spots around three major Soldier structures – the general store, the school, and the Pilgrim Holiness church.

Mabel and Thurman's house is about eight feet from the general store. Post office, food, non-prescription pharmacy, some clothing - it's all there. Harlan and I always charge the milk and bread like we're going to pay for it ourselves someday.

The school, grades one through six, stands high on the hill with its

Soldier School Reunion 1991

back to the community, but welcoming to those that make it up that steep one-lane dirt road.

"The next year I was placed in Soldier to teach first grade for one half day and freshman spelling and farm management in the afternoon. I taught J.R. in the first grade there. I can remember him smelling so clean. He wore the cutest outfits and every hair was in place. J. R. grew up and married my half-sister Patty. "Baby" Ray Conley was my student in the first grade. He was a big boy and chewed tobacco. He would climb up the school hill and throw out his tobacco just as he entered."

Harlan and I attend Sunday School regularly at the Pilgrim Holiness, but never stay for Church services. Baptisms are held below the church in the unnamed creek, which is waist deep in one small area that is big enough for two people.

HAYWARD

Soldier, Enterprise, and Lawton would be considered "destination" communities. Hayward, on the other hand, like Haldeman and Limestone, are pass-through communities, meaning that unless you have a reason to stop, you won't.

Hayward sleepily sits a little less than a mile down the road from Soldier, not a stitch of life between them. Hayward's one community feels more like three, because of the way it is laid out, and because of the two soft s-curves that perfectly divide it. Each section stands alone, but each is unquestionably dependent on the other two.

Section one visually challenges you from the backseat. Straight ahead is the first s-curve and the best glimpse into the Hayward brick plant. To the right, the Hayward general store stands on the corner next to a mid-50s cul-de-sac alley dotted with a few motel cabin-size houses. I've never been in that store, but I have been told that Mom Davis once lived in one of those houses beside it.

On the left, just far enough off the road to stretch your neck, the parallel creek and railroad visually lead your eyes up to the Clark Cemetery. Even though the graves correctly face the rising sun, they are unfortunately plotted on a steep north-south sloping hill. The hill is so steep that gravity has probably rolled the departed relatives to their right side, negating the "graves must face east" protocol. Dad's side of the family is buried in the Clark Cemetery. We visit them regularly each Memorial Day and decorate their graves.

Hayward's second section is the brick plant. Built in 1900, the plant produces anywhere from 12,000 to 15,000 bricks per day. The fire clay mine that feeds the plant is located high above and behind the brickyard. Clyde Hayward, an employee of the Ashland Fire Brick Company, built the plant and gave the community its namesake.

"Cooge started work at the plant at age 15. He lied and said he was 16. It did not matter until he started to retire and had to work an extra year. They held his position when he entered service for World War II. The union had been formed and he was making good money. He could tell some scary stories about when they began organizing the union. There were carts overturned, bricks thrown, houses burned, and work stoppages ordered. He worked by quota piece. Sometimes he would have his day's work done by 9 am."

Unlike in Haldeman, the Hayward kilns are away from the road. The view of the plant from the road is obscured by a small ridge that runs the length of the plant. Within seconds of clearing that first s-curve, you are past the plant's entrance and facing Hayward's second s-curve and third community section – the company housing.

Six to eight houses dot both sides of the road just before and after that soft curve. These houses are owned by the company and rented

Davis Company House

to employees. I was born in 1947 and our family lived in one of these homes until the early 50s.

"When we moved into the company house, it had to be renovated. I had the floors cleaned, and Esther and I papered the crooked walls. There were linoleum rugs on the floors and new furniture. Cooge even built a fence around the property. The fence was crooked, and several men at the plant asked him for a blueprint. There was a whistle that blew at the plant at four in the morning that meant get out of bed and get ready for work at six. The whistle was loud enough to be heard for miles. We would bank the fire the night before, and it was still very cold when you hit the floor. Then you had to warm the kitchen before you could break the ice for water to cook. I would fry meat and eggs, then make gravy and biscuits and pack his lunch. After he walked to the plant I would have time to do some housework and get ready to walk to school."

Driving along the two s-curves, from the Davis family cemetery to the last company house, takes all of about 25 seconds. Most people assume that Hayward is a drive-by community half-way between Soldier and Enterprise – a place where memories only count if you live or work there. They are right.

ENTERPRISE

A lot of life has been lived here. If you're family you start to feel your heritage long before you see it. Our family roots are planted deep in Enterprise.

The Enterprise community is less than a mile from Hayward. Among the six communities, Enterprise is where the road, rail tracks, and creek run the closest to each other. For locals, crossing them isn't a rarity, just a way of life. Geographically, Enterprise is short, about two dozen heartbeats. But it is long enough to fashion the local vocabulary around such terms as "home-place, down in the Bottom, over home, up the road, across the tracks, across the creek, and down the holler."

"Enterprise was a small place, but at that time there was the depot, two grocery stores, a post office and a barber shop. Trains ran east and west each day. There was a restaurant also, because that's where I met Cooge."

The depot was the center of the community before it was torn down in the early 50s. It sat between the road and the tracks and transitioned people from one form of transportation to another. Retail was across the road and in front of the creek. The

Patty Hall

businesses shriveled like unpicked grapes when the trains stopped coming. But post-war, they were fine wine.

"I had been to the post office and stopped in the restaurant to buy a Coke. There were some guys in the back, so I ambled back to play the juke box. I put my nickel in, and Donnie Tackett quickly chose another number. I said, "Donnie Tackett!" and this soldier stood up and pulled a nickel from his pocket and said, "Play what you want to, pretty lady." Well, that did it. Cooge walked me home and had to hold me on the swinging bridge crossing the creek. He held me for the rest of his life."

Right before the depot on the left runs a dirt lane across the tracks and back into a holler. There sits the Enterprise school.

"When the fall term began I went to teach at Enterprise. I taught Betty, Kathaleen, and Barbara. I had the building wired for electric, had the floors cleaned and painted, painted desks, and built an extra room for hot lunches. We had a gas stove and hired a cook. There were pie suppers and square dances; and people in the community helped."

Just before the depot and to the right is a treeless hill that falls gradually from its tree line at the top to the creek bed below. On that piece of ground stands the "home place," where parents parent and children listen. It is here that Stewart, Stella, Esther, Mom, Marge, Jack, Kathaleen, Betty, and even Billy, Patty, Allen, and Barbara created family memories.

Stewart built a new house "down in the Bottom." I define "Bottom" as any physical place away from and lower than the "home place." In actuality, the Bottom and its brand new home is about a sniper's shot down 174 from the depot. Stewart built another house on the north side of the tracks near the depot area, and moved in what family had not moved on. After all the Hall family shuffling, the Davis family moved from Hayward to the "Bottom" home.

"We moved from Hayward to Enterprise. We rented from Dad and had so much more room. The boys had a pet chicken left over from Easter. It was in a pen in the back lawn. One morning we decided to kill the chicken for Sunday dinner. Cooge had taken them to Sunday School, and I slowly prepared to ring that chicken's neck. I can't remember why, but they came home early and were standing on the back porch when I finished wringing the neck. The chicken went flopping across the lawn, and they began to scream. Those two boys did not love me or their dad for weeks after that."

Harlan and I rode our bicycles to the Enterprise general store and back for milk and bread, as we would do later in Soldier. The creek was across the road from the "Bottom" house where we helped Mom and Dad wash the car. About 50 yards down the creek bed there was a sharp turn in the creek that created a nice little swimming hole for the two of us. No lifeguard, no lap swimming, neither of us could spell chlorine or cared how to bring our "swimming pool" into today's balance. However, we did wear shoes because of the rocky bottom and watched out for the occasional snake.

Harlan and I have talked about it and we agree that we loved our time at the "Bottom."

LAWTON

If Lawton was a mineral, it would be gold: rich and rare, hard and cold. If Lawton was a food it would be an onion: layers of history that can make you cry.

Lawton lays just a mile and a half from Enterprise. Route 174 uncharacteristically straightens out just before Lawton hits you like a slap in the face. And, like that slap in the face, it's over quickly because Lawton is not about length, it's all about depth.

Lawton IS the Rayburn store, built in 1889. It's big. It's red and white. It's right there off the road, close as kin. Its position between the road and the railroad tracks lets it double as a store in front and a depot in back. Car and train passengers alike can be inside the building within a matter of seconds. The store is run by the Rayburn family, a family with seemingly more branches on its family tree than all the real trees in Carter County.

Once you pass the store on Route 174, you've pretty much passed Lawton. All the action in Lawton, past and present, runs down the side road that starts next to the store. That little two-lane road immediately runs

Time has not been kind to the store

over the tracks and off to a world not usually shown to children. That road then branches into a series of arterial roads that run off in many directions, even going as far down as Elliott County.

You can follow those arteries to the limestone caves atop the hills behind the store. Their gaping entrances have for decades swallowed hundreds of workers each morning only to spit them out later in the day. You can also follow those arteries to the mushroom mines, where the local gossip is about satanic rituals being performed on certain nights of the year.

At one time, Lawton had a movie theatre. Churches and families

Lawton Pentecostal Church 1920

dotted the landscape like freckles on a red-headed child. Life in Lawton in the mid 50s seemed like more of an afterthought compared to decades past. Even as a child, I could feel that my experience in Lawton was only the outer skin of the onion, and that Lawton's real story requires many peelings. Between those layers are thousands of golden stories, some hard and cold, many bright and promising. Unfortunately, most of them will stay hidden.

"My father was working on the railroad, and in his position as a section boss he could ride the train when necessary. When a train stopped in Lawton once for freight and passengers, Dad looked up and saw this beautiful lady with a red hat and a silver pin. He boarded the train, and in talking to her was able to secure her name and address. She became my Mom. Jack and I were born in Lawton, but in different houses."

Further down Route 174, past the Rayburn store and around a gentle curve, there is a wide silver gate guarding a steep hill. The treasure is not the hill itself but the Fielding Cemetery at its top. The cemetery is hard to find, hard to get to, and hard to maintain. Buried here are branches of the Hall and Fielding family trees. The graves face east but the ever-expanding trees keep the sun from hitting the interred until about noon. The real view is to the right: a battered fence does its best to keep the roaming animals at bay.

There are hundreds of family cemeteries in Carter County. Each cemetery tells wonderful family stories, but generally leaves more questions than answers. Our family cemetery is no exception. Whether you walk up the hill for safety, or chance the deep gullies by car, you'll come down scratching your head; I promise.

LIMESTONE

Limestone is listed as one of Route 174's ghost town social communities. However, this may be a figment of a deceased map-maker's twisted imagination. Limestone is grouped with the other five communities because it shows up on maps, just like New York City and LA.

Limestone is only three curves away from the cemetery gate, but you might miss it if you blink. One could easily question its reality. Haldeman, Soldier, Hayward, Enterprise, and Lawton are real: real people, real stories. As a kid of 12, Limestone existed only in my mind. As an adult, it still does.

Limestone has two road signs that say "Limestone." As soon as you pass the Limestone corporation sign going east, quickly turn around and you will see the Limestone corporation sign as if you were going west. Depending on the driver's speed, you could pass Limestone without even knowing it. Whoever put those signs up could have saved some money and put the name on both sides of one sign, saving the other sign for later use.

Personally, I think Limestone was a ghost town long before it became a ghost town. There is one house, a small church, and a road between the two signs. The promise of Limestone has to be down that road, one never traveled by me. The rumor is that Porter Creek is down there somewhere, along with something that has to do with limestone. Let's hope so.

But, ghost towns come in all sizes. The uniting thread that runs through each ghost town is the fact that it existed in the first place. Limestone pushes that envelope for me. Go figure.

Family.

The communities I knew on Route 174 in post World War II Kentucky were active and thriving communities. I sensed, but didn't realize at the time, how far on the backside of their heyday they really were.

A community becomes a ghost town once the economic activity that supported it decreases significantly. The communities of Route 174 are still populated, not abandoned like some western tumbleweed town we see in a movie. The people that live in and around these communities these days spend their lives just like my family did during and before my youth – moving forward, one day at a time.

Such push back grit found on Route 174 and throughout Carter County, then and now, would be welcome in a lot of communities today across this country.

Davis/Hall

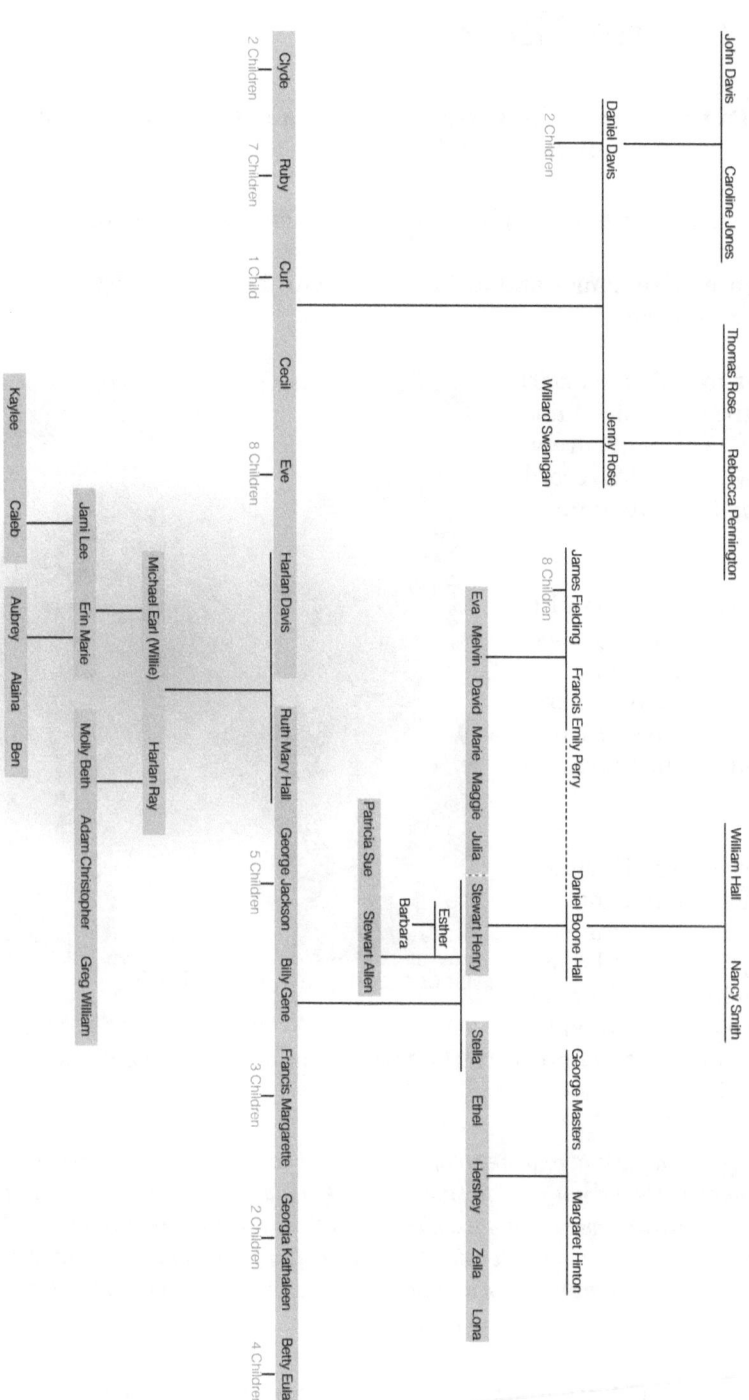

Flesh and Blood

"What's in a name? That which we call a rose by any other name would smell as sweet."

Shakespeare's Juliet thought so. I, on the other hand, am not so sure.

There are more names and nicknames in our family than drunks on St. Patrick's Day.

There's me, Michael Earl, later given the nickname "Willie." This will surely confuse all official record keeping far beyond my death.

My brother is Harlan Ray. The "Ray" was only used by those friends and relatives who lived south of the Ohio River. Also at a high pitch when Mom was mad at him.

Our father was Harlan. No official middle name, but plenty of nicknames: Cooge, "The Kid." I don't know why Mom shunned protocol and endowed the

Cooge and Ruth, about 1965

second son, not the first, with the father's name. We joked about that later in life.

"Cooge loved me and told me so often. When I became pregnant, he became very unhappy. He did not want to share me with a baby. I was 21 and wanted 12 children. He was 33 and did not want to start a family. Harlan was conceived by a lot of hard work and a little deceit. But, he was a good father to those two boys. Cooge was proud of them. Both of them called him Cooge until they started school."

Our mother was Ruth Mary. She had a laundry list of names

throughout her life: Ruth Hall Davis, Ruth Mary Hall Davis, Ruth Mary Hall Fielding Davis, Mrs. Harlan Davis, Mrs. Cooge Davis, as well as the odd "Oocher."

Our fraternal grandfather was Daniel Davis. Daniel was born in Wales, Great Britain in 1855, five years before Lincoln became President. He fathered Cooge at age 56. He then fathered five more children over the next 11 years with Jenny, 32 years his junior.

Our fraternal grandmother was Jenny Rose. Jenny married Mr. Swanigan, had a son Willard by him, and then divorced him. She married Daniel at age 24. She was always referred to as Mom Davis.

"Mom Davis and Willard were living with us when Mike was born. Mom did not really like Mr. Davis. He liked the women and was not a good provider. Mom Davis was always saying negative things about him."

Our maternal grandfather was Stewart Henry. Stewart was a Perry, became a Fielding, and then, a Hall. He carried the nickname "Preacher." Stewart's mother was Francis Perry, who became a Fielding. Stewart's father was Daniel Hall, who gave himself the middle name Boone because it sounded cool. You go guy!

Our maternal grandmother was Stella. She was a Masters before becoming a Hall. Stella had four sisters who all dropped the Masters name when they married. The sisters were all Aunts to our mother and, therefore, she called them Aunt (insert name here), and so did we.

"Aunt Ethel tried so hard to make a lady of me. She made me walk with books on my head, taught me to set a table, and taught me the importance of having good silver, china, and crystal. Aunt Zella came to visit me in Soldier. She had married seven times. She raised canaries and rabbits for pet shops. Aunt Lona and Walter Day had four children. One of them, James, had polio. He became (I think) editor of the Ashland newspaper."

Our maternal step-grandmother was Esther. She was an Evans, then a Saylers, and then a Hall. Esther had a previous daughter who became a Wells. Stewart had two children, Patricia

Allen Hall

Sue, who married a Vincent, and Allen, who has always stood tall as a Hall.

Harlan Ray and I have 12 family only aunts and uncles, not counting spouses and Mom's four aunts. There was Aunt Margarette, Aunt Kathaleen, Uncle Jack, Aunt Betty, Aunt Patty, Uncle Allen, Uncle Willard, Aunt Eve, Aunt Ruby, Uncle Curt, Uncle Cecil, Uncle Clyde.

As can be expected, aunts marry and change their last names. Our Hall and Davis Aunts became a Sagraves, Schnitzer, Mabry, Pickens, Bradley, Walker, Vincent, Day, and Knipp. Uncles remained a Hall, Davis, or Swanigan. Our Aunt and Uncle marriages produced 32 cousins and a slew of first and second cousins once removed.

Names are just flesh and blood labels. However it's hearts that bind them into families. I think ours was such a family.

"I was trying to take Mom's place after she died. I would try and prepare Dad's breakfast and pack his lunch. I was always carrying Betty on my hip. I slept between Betty and Kathaleen. I rubbed Betty's leg and let Kathaleen pull on my ear."

Aunt Zell

Aunt Ethel, Mom and the boys

The Davis Family

Daniel and Jennie

Together Wales, Scotland and England form Great Britain. Davis is a Wales surname. John W. brought it with him when he immigrated to America in the first half of the 19th century. He settled in Ruddells Mills, Bourbon County, Kentucky, about 30 miles northeast of Lexington. There he met Caroline Jones from Millersburg, just a hop, skip and a jump away. On July 12th, 1855 they had a son, Daniel Davis, my grandfather.

Daniel Davis

Franklin Pierce was President when Daniel was born. Abraham Lincoln was a small town lawyer in Illinois. Robert E. Lee was biding his time as an obscure second in command of a cavalry regiment in Texas. Slavery and its expansion or abolition was the heated argument of the day.

Daniel Davis was my oldest grandfather. It is rare that a front-bumper baby boomer like me would have a grandfather that was born two years before the Supreme Court decided Dred Scott had no right to be a US citizen.

In 1889, Jenny Rose was born in Carter County to Thomas Rose and Rebecca Pennington. Daniel was 34 at the time. Around 20 years later, they met and married. Daniel was 56 at the time and had been married twice, siring two known sons, Justice and Keaton. Jenny was not a Rose then, but a Swanigan, and already had son, Willard, from her previous marriage. Daniel and Jenny started another branch of the Davis family in 1911 by producing the first of their six children, Harlan. Harlan was my dad.

Daniel was a day laborer, farmer, clay mine and brick plant worker, and circuit preacher. He appears to also have been a smooth talker and rabbit prolific. For all we know, every Davis in Kentucky may be related. Not surprisingly, Daniel died in May of 1933 from a malfunctioning heart valve. He is buried in the Clark Cemetery in Hayward.

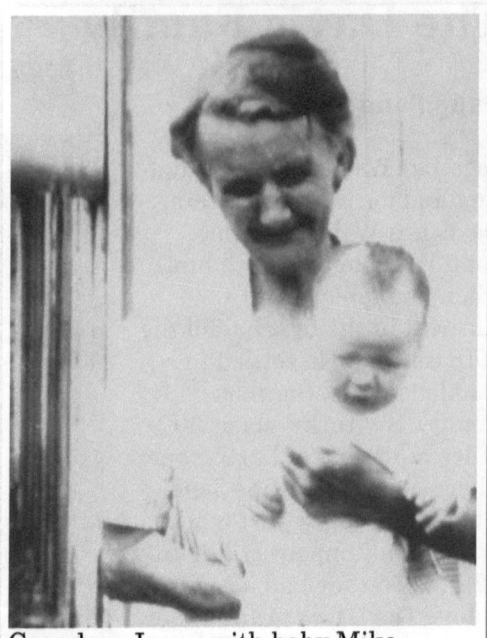

Grandma Jenny with baby Mike

"Cooge's father died and left a charged bill at Sam Hamm's grocery store. Cooge had to pay that bill and take care of the family. His father seemed never to be home. Cooge's mother would tell some terrible stories of how they lived. She caught him with another woman one time and threw a bucket of water on them."

Jenny died in 1948, at the age of 59. I was just one at the time, and Harlan Ray was not yet born. Jenny is buried beside Daniel in Hayward.

Cooge.

Our dad Harlan had two nicknames – "Cooge" and "The Kid." Cooge stuck when Dad was a baby and one of his family members rubbed his chin and said, "coochee, coochee, coochee." The Kid came later, when Mom Davis sent Dad to the grocery store to buy some bologna.

Cooge "The Kid" at Hayward

On his way there, Dad stopped at Becky Salyers' house, where one of her pretty daughters taught Dad a thing or two about life. He never got to the bologna, and when one of the men at the brick plant called him the "Bologna Kid," it stuck and eventually evolved into "The Kid."

Dad was born in Lawton on December 26, 1911. It seems that everybody in Carter County is somehow tied to Lawton. Having only completed the fifth grade, Dad lied about his age and got a job at the brick plant in Hayward, to help support Mom Davis, Eve, Ruby, Curt, Cecil, and Clyde. He was only 15.

He worked at the plant for 31 years until it closed in 1957. He, like so many other men, left his work to fight in World War II. He trained for 10 months stateside before being shipped to Scotland in 1943. He landed in Normandy, Omaha Beach, on June 6th and was wounded around St. Lo on July 12th. After being hospitalized in England for three months, he spent another three months in a US hospital, before being honorably discharged with a Purple Heart and Bronze Star. For the rest of his life, he had that zipper-like scar on his left arm, caused by an exploding shell that almost took his life.

Dad was a poker player. He flat-out loved to play cards.

"When Cooge walked me home that first time from the restaurant, Dad said, "What are you doing here Kid?" Dad knew him from playing poker. I found out later he was a card shark. You wouldn't believe how he could shuffle cards or deal himself cards up a sleeve. He never had enough patience with me and the boys. One time Cooge took Michael for a drive while I stayed with our new baby, Harlan Ray. After dark I became worried and sought help from a neighbor. Betty Gee walked to Enterprise and found Mike at Esther's. Cooge had decided to play poker with the guys. Esther had no option other than to change Mike into a dishtowel. On our first wedding anniversary I prepared a good meal, lit a candle, and dressed appropriately. Cooge did not come in until 5 am. He brought a friend with him to pave the way. The back door opened and $500 was thrown in first. There were a lot of problems with drinking and poker."

Mom and Dad met in the spring after Dad's February discharge from the service. The war in Europe had ended, and the war in the Pacific would last another few months. They were married in December of 1945, three days before Dad's 34th birthday.

"I can't remember whose car he was driving one Sunday afternoon when he took me up Limestone Hollow. He told me to put out or get out. I got out and started walking. He drove away but came back and asked me to marry him. I said yes, and we rode the bus to Ashland the next day and were married. We spent the first

Dad traveled to Mansfield and found work with Borg-Warner when the North American Refractories brick plant closed in Hayward. He stayed with Aunt Kathaleen for over a year and drove back and forth to Soldier on the weekends. Mom, Harlan, and I joined him in 1959 and the four of us began our Ohio life together in Ontario.

He had a heart attack in 1970 and eventually died of heart disease on January 2nd, 1972, at the age of 61. He is buried in the Fielding Cemetery at Lawton.

Aunts, Uncles, and Cousins

Dad's two sisters, Eve and Ruby, married and lived locally. Eve married Willard Day and they first lived in Soldier and then Morehead. Willard was called Booger, and I have always thought it odd that multiple names with double Os showed up twice in our family, Cooge and Booge.

I also find it interesting that three of the four brothers' names begin with a C, and the one that doesn't, Harlan, became a Cooge. Curt, Clyde, Cecil, and Cooge. Sounds like a vaudeville act.

Eve holding Clyde

Eve, born in 1914, and Booger had eight children, Norma, Jimmy, Maggie, Don, Bobby, Ruth, Gayle, and Wendell. Ruth was my age and Wendell was Harlan's age. We visited them often in Soldier, but less in Morehead.

Ruby, born in 1920, married Arthur Knipp. They lived in Enterprise and had seven children, Patty, Ernest, Sharon, Larry, Frank, Daniel, and Joan Earline. Larry and Harlan were the same age and, even today, stay in touch and play golf together at least once a year.

"Because Cooge was the oldest, he was forever in the middle of a dispute with one of his brothers or sisters. They consulted him, but usually did not take his advice. Once Ruby knocked on the door in the middle of the night. She told him

some story as to why Arthur had thrown her out of the house. Cooge went down the next day to talk to Arthur and Arthur shot at him."

Dad's two brothers, Curt and Clyde, both moved out of state.

Curt, born in 1918, married Leona Lewis and they lived in Indiana. They had one daughter, Susan. We saw very little of them, however, they did visit us from time to time. I remember Curt as tall, Leona small, and Susan cute. Curt was a real cut up with an oddball sense of humor. He visited us in Mansfield once and we played a round of golf. As a left hander, he wasn't bad. I remember thinking that I should have known him better.

"Curt and Leona came to visit, and he and Cooge were drinking. The next morning, Curt could not get out of bed because of a hangover. When he did arise he vomited on the wall, bed, and floor. He was so embarrassed, and Cooge laughed at him and called him a sissy. Leona spent the morning cleaning up the mess, and then they left early for Indiana."

Clyde, the youngest of the family, was born in 1923. Clyde married Darlene and they had two children, Carolyn Sue and Rodger. Clyde was quiet like Dad, but Darlene was feisty and always a ball to be around. They lived in Mansfield and my memories of them are there.

Cousin Rodger

"Clyde and Darlene came to visit once, and they were drinking. She pulled a gun from her purse and threatened to shoot the two of them."

Cecil, born in 1915, died in 1954 in a hunting accident. I was six at the time of his death, and I do not remember Cecil at all. I seem to know even less about him now.

Upon first look, a mix of 10 aunts and uncles, 18 cousins, and a few of

Mom's scattered wild memories, seems like a Davis family circus. This is certainly not the case. Although there were no Sunday reunions where everyone brought a covered dish, there were lots of tight-knit individual family visits where the kids played while the adults shared life's ups and downs.

All my "Davis side of the family" memories are pleasant ones. It was always obvious that all of Dad's family treated him with respect. All our cousins, even our older cousins, were kind to Harlan and I.

Looking back now, I wish I had spent more time with them.

The Hall Family

Daniel Boone Hall

I have never known of any other man to just give himself a middle name. "When I started growing up I just sort of added the Boone to Daniel," said the 96 year old veteran in a 1970 newspaper article.

My Great-Grandfather, Daniel "Boone" Hall, was born one or two counties south of Carter the day after Christmas, 1874. Ulysses S. Grant was President at the time, while Jesse James was robbing trains in Missouri.

Daniel joined in the anti-Spain frenzy and became a Spanish-American War veteran when the war ended in 1898. Upon

Daniel Boone Hall

returning to Kentucky, the 26-year-old Daniel met a 24-year-old Francis Emily Perry. They had a son out of wedlock, my grandfather Stewart Henry in 1901.

Young children don't hear all the details, but, as the story goes, Daniel rode off into the sunset before Stewart was even born. He grew some roots in the Pacific Northwest where he had some relatives, and started a family there. Francis, abandoned with a son and left to fend for herself, met and married an older James Fielding who had previously fathered eight children with a Sara and a Sue. Stewart, who was three at the time, became a Fielding and a half-brother to the six children Francis and James produced thereafter. Whew!

Many years later, Daniel left his West Coast life behind and headed back to Kentucky to find Stewart. Stewart and his half-brothers and sisters were adults by now, and their mother Francis, and Stewart's step-father, James Fielding, had passed away. Stewart Henry was a Fielding until Daniel Boone showed up. He then became Stewart Hall.

"One day a train pulled in, and Dad's real father arrived. He asked at the depot for Dad, and people took one look, and then said he owned a grocery store across the street. They looked exactly like each other. Grandpa's story was that he went off to war and made a different life for himself. He ended up married and living out West. I know he had grown children because he talked of a rift in the family that made him decide to leave and find the child he had left in Kentucky. He had really searched until he found Dad. He moved into our house."

As a child, I thought Daniel Boone Hall was like Casper the Ghost. Here today, gone tomorrow. He had family in Wrigley and seemed to bounce back and forth quite often between there and Enterprise. He died in the early 1970s at the age of 96. He's buried in West Liberty.

I'm sure there are enough Daniel Boone Hall stories to fill a small library. I remember him as a quiet, cane bearing, tobacco chewing elder that loved to whittle. I don't think anybody ever made Daniel Boone Hall do anything he didn't want to do. The independence streak that runs in the Hall family can surely be traced back to my great-grandfather.

Stewart, Stella, and Esther

Stewart, my grandfather, was called Preacher by most people; he was known as Preacher Fielding.

"The nickname Preacher stuck one afternoon when Dad was riding a horse, when his shirttail came out and was flying in the wind. One of his friends called out. 'Watch that preacher's tail fly.' The name stuck."

It must have been confusing when Preacher Fielding suddenly became Stewart Hall. I'm sure many people did not know a Stewart Hall, but did know a Preacher Fielding. Stella, his first wife and my Grandmother, married him when he was still Stewart Fielding. Their six children, my aunts and uncles, were all Fieldings as children and Halls as adults. Undoubtedly, there are many stories around this confusing name change.

I knew Stewart Hall Preacher Fielding as Papa. He was always a quiet man to me, but there was a big stick around which he had used in his past. His life was on Route 174, in Lawton, Soldier, Hayward, and Enterprise. He was a conductor on the railroad, supervisor at a sand plant up on Peter Cave Hollow, and owned the grocery store at Enterprise for years..

"In 1934, Dad was burned in a gasoline explosion at the Sand Plant. He was filling a tram car with gasoline, and he was the only person there. The engine exploded and Dad tried to jump out of the window. His overall bib caught and he hung there and his clothes burned before he could fall to the ground. He was taken to King Daughter's hospital in Ashland and suffered from extensive burns. He was in the hospital for a long time."

At age 22, in 1923, he married Stella Masters, three years his senior. They met while Stella was living in Indiana and visiting her parents who lived in Flat Fork. Their life together was on Route 174, Lawton, Hayward, Soldier, and Enterprise. They had six children, all born in the home.

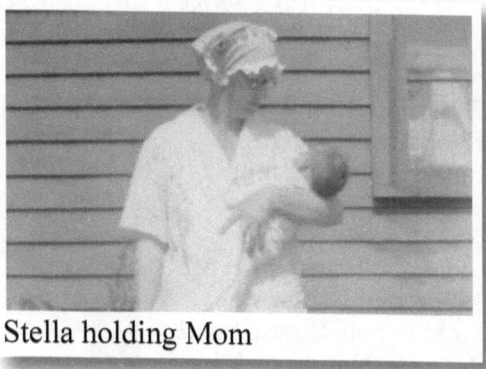

Stella holding Mom

"Jack and I were both born in Lawton but in different houses. Margaret was born in Hayward, Kathaleen and Betty in Enterprise. I don't know where Billy was born."

All six children were born within a nine year span. Ruth, my mom and the oldest of the six, was born in 1924, while Betty Eulane, the youngest, was born in 1933. Billy Gene was born in 1928 and died at the age of four of diphtheria.

"When Billy was ill, Mom holding him and crying is a vivid memory. She was urging Dad to hurry for the doctor. This was after dark, and we were all in bed. Dad had to walk to Soldier, and he returned in a horse and buggy that belonged to Dr. Logan. Billy had died by then."

According to Mom, Preacher and Stella's marriage was not always a Valentine's Day. Stella stood toe-to-toe with the Hall independent streak, so they clashed many times. The marriage lasted 12 years, as Stella died in 1935.

"Mom's death and stories about the cause have changed over the years. The

original story and what Aunt Julia repeated later was a blood clot on the brain
after stomach surgery. I know she had bleeding when she went to the toilet
because I can remember seeing the blood. Dad was sitting by her side after
surgery when she asked for a sip of water. She was not to raise her head, much
less sit up. She drank the water and laid back down, and in a few minutes was
pronounced dead. I am sure in this day and time her life would have been
saved."

"Dad made a mistake on Mom's tombstone. The date was wrong, or I was a
bastard. There was a quiet discussion as to who was to go home with whom after
the burial. We had some aunts who wanted us, but we have to give Dad credit
for keeping us together."

Everyone fell in love with Esther when she came into the Fielding family, especially Stewart. The term "hired girl" was colloquial language in the 1930s, and Esther was hired to help Stewart with the girls. Nature took its course, and on Mom's 16th birthday Preacher and Esther were married.

Esther was about 17 years Preacher's junior, and only about six years older than Mom. Esther was raised as an Evans in Hayward, divorced from Bert Salyers, and had a

Esther and Stewart

daughter, Barbara, when she started working for Preacher. She married into a household of five children, brought in one of her own, and mothered two more with Stewart, Patty and Allen. You go girl.

Esther was one of the kindest ladies I ever knew. In retrospect, I think she was also one of the most resilient. Even though Preacher seemed to have mellowed with age, longtime household resident Daniel Boone Hall probably didn't. Preacher's four daughters had vastly different personalities, and Esther's three children each had their own challenges as well. All the children grew up, married, and had children. Some divorced and remarried. Those children had children. Esther always seemed to know who was who, who was where, and some inside truths about each one.

For her entire life, she bounced more balls and memories in the air than a circus clown could imagine – with better grace and dignity.

"When we moved into the company house in Hayward, it had to be renovated. I had the floors cleaned, and Esther and I papered the crooked walls. When we were papering the back bedroom, we caught the kitchen on fire. I had put the tea kettle on to boil water to make paste. I had turned on the wrong burner and went back to talk with her. We laughed later, because we had just papered the kitchen and had to do it over again."

Ruth Mary

My Mom. She inherited every independent DNA strand the Hall family lineage could muster. She had drive. She was strong and firm, an air of hardness about her when she needed to show it. She was also compassionate, sensitive, and sympathetic, although few people saw that tender side of her.

To the outside world, she came across as an Appalachian Rosy the Riveter with an attitude. To Harlan and me, she was June Cleaver and Harriet Nelson on steroids. To Dad, I think, she was an anchor that kept his boat inside the still waters.

Mom at Hayward

Although she was only eleven or twelve when her Mom passed away, she was old enough to realize that she had just assumed some added responsibilities, since Kathaleen was three and Betty was two.

"I was trying to take Mom's place. I would try to prepare Dad's breakfast and pack his lunch. I can remember putting cups of something in his lunch bucket. I wonder what it was."

Mom attended Enterprise for her elementary schooling, and then a private Methodist boarding school in high school – Erie School in Olive Hill. She completed Erie in three years and began her 17-year Morehead College career at age 15.

Erie School

Mom's roommate at Morehead was Elizabeth McGuire, who she became close friends with for years. Elizabeth's brother Heman was the Carter County superintendent when the war broke out. The war created a shortage of teachers and he asked both Mom and Elizabeth to teach with a temporary certificate.

Rattlesnake School

"I was just 16. My first teaching assignment was Rattlesnake School back of Grahn. When building the school, they unearthed a nest of rattlesnakes. The school was down in the valley and could only be reached by walking, horseback, or horse and wagon. Dad would take me to the top of the ridge, and Mr. Carrol would meet me with the wagon. I was only out of there two times during the school year. All eight grades were in one room. Mrs. Carrol boarded the teachers for $13 per month. I made $65 and saved enough to go back to college in the spring."

In the fall, Mom was transferred from Rattlesnake to Enterprise where she taught Betty, Kathaleen, and Barbara. She was transferred to Soldier to teach the next year, and continued teaching there until we moved to Mansfield in 1959. By age 35, Mom had been teaching for about half of her life without a college degree. Nevertheless, she was constantly taking summer courses at Morehead while balancing her work, marriage, and parenting. She graduated from Morehead in 1958.

The Women's Rights movement had a full head of steam during

Mom's childhood, and her Aunt Julia, Preacher's half-sister, was a strong advocate for women's education. Aunt Julia was a teacher in Ashland and pushed Preacher hard to support Mom's formal education. Julia also served as Mom's role model.

"Aunt Julia and Uncle Earl had a house full of laughter. They were both comedians and would laugh at each other. They would take us for rides in their car with the rumble seat. Some of the roads followed the creek beds. It was so much fun to go down into the water and up to the other side."

Aunt Ethel, Stella's sister, also served as Mom's role model.

"The summer before I met Cooge I stayed with Aunt Ethel in Indiana and worked in a defense plant. I was on the evening shift, working on an assembly line. I sat on a stool and painted a red mark on land mines. Some woman asked me when I started wearing shoes because I was from Kentucky. I slapped her and we had a fight on the floor. Aunt Ethel taught me to walk like a lady, or she thought so. One Sunday we went to church and I was all dressed up with hose, hat, and high heels. When we reached the curb, I did not step down and sprawled into the street. She was so disappointed. She took me home and started walking lessons all over again."

Mom had lots of suitors. There was Esther's brother Allan, then Ralph Stevens, Charlie Rice, Elmer King, and George Sealy. And then Mom fell for Alton Ray Coohen. "Cooney" was a Navy man and proposed to Mom through the mail. Mom said yes, but he was killed in action in the Pacific.

Ultimately, it was Cooge who won Mom's heart for real.

Cooge, Ruth and the boys

"I dated Cooge and was impressed with the way he spent money. We went

everywhere in a taxi, and I thought he had money. After we were married, he brought his change of underwear and three shirts to the marriage."

When our family moved to Mansfield, Mom accepted a contract from Ontario. She taught first, third, and fifth grades there for almost 20 years before retiring. Add those to her almost 20 years of teaching in Kentucky, and you have a lot of students who learned to read and write from Mrs. Davis.

Mom passed away in May of 1994 and is buried next to Dad in the Fielding Cemetery in Lawton.

Aunts, Uncles, and Cousins

Aunt Kathaleen and her family were living and working in Mansfield during my youth in Kentucky. She married Rolland Mabry, in 1950, and had two sons: Ron and Dennis. The first time I saw Dennis was when Kat brought him to the Fielding Cemetery one Memorial Day. She had him wrapped in her arms and had walked up the entire hill holding him.

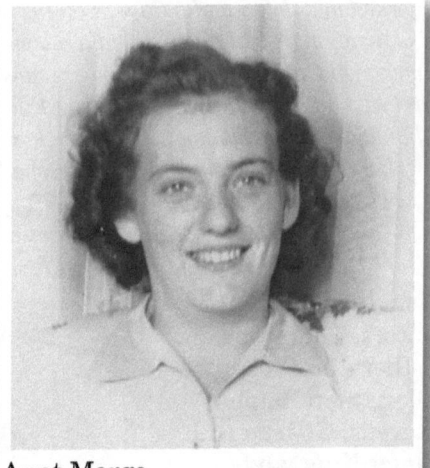
Aunt Marge

Aunt Marge lived in West Virginia and was married to Herman. They had three children: Woody, Sybil, and James. They occasionally came to visit, but mostly we saw them once a year at Camden Park in Huntington at Herman's annual company picnic.

Aunt Betty lived in Columbus, Ohio was married to Albert Bradley, and had a son, William Edward. That marriage didn't work out and Betty eventually married Bud Walker, a rancher at heart. He moved Aunt

Aunt Betty

Betty and their three daughters, Valerie, Trula, and JoAnna, to Antlers, Oklahoma. Later on, in the 70s, Mom drove Marge, Esther, and Preacher to Oklahoma to see Betty. I'll bet that was some trip!

Barbara also lived in Ohio. She married Cecil Wells and had two daughters: Joni and Vicki. I became closer with Aunt Barbara later on in life.

Jack stayed in Enterprise, but we didn't see much of him or his family. Jack was a disabled veteran. After his military service he worked locally, married Jewell Flannery, and they had five children: Daniel, Lewis, Billy, Brenda, and Barry. While in the Philippines he fathered two daughters, Pilar Ruth and Lillian. Later in life, Pilar traced her father and visited his gravesite. Mom loved everyone in her family, but she especially loved Jack. However, she spoke little about him.

Patty and Allen were more like cousins than an aunt and uncle. Patty was born in 1941 and Allen was born in 1944. When the Davis family went north in 1959, Patty was in her prime as a teenager. She was attracting boys to Enterprise

Michael, Allen, Esther and Harlan

like bees to honey. She eventually married J.R. Vincent and they had a daughter, Jill Reneé. Unfortunately, J.R. was killed in an automobile accident in 1977.

Allen was only three years older than me, and five years older than Harlan. I remember Allen and me teaming up against the young pup in a rock throwing contest. Unfortunately for Harlan, the rocks were at each other and we caused a cut over Harlan's eye. I regret that to this day. Allen later became the Kentucky John Henry of the railroad, married Bonnie, and had a son Dwayne.

Therefore, at the time of our Ohio move, Harlan and I had 10 aunts and uncles and 14 cousins on Mom's side of the family. Add that to Dad's side of the family and there were a total of 20 aunts and uncles and 32 cousins in our collective memory bank.

The branches on the Davis/Hall family tree were numerous even back in 1959. They have grown even more since then.

Harlan Ray birthday party

Aunt Julia with Mom

Hodgepodge

...Julia and Earl were close to our family. Since they were Mom's aunt and uncle, therefore, they became Aunt Julia and Uncle Earl to Harlan and me.

"When Mike was born, Uncle Earl rode the train from Ashland to Hayward and walked in a deep snow to the house to give me a beautiful blue shawl. I named my first baby, Michael Earl, after my Uncle Earl."

Aunt Julia and Uncle Earl

We traveled to Ashland often on Sunday afternoons to visit them. I was the ring bearer at their son Roy Earl's wedding. I had a black eye at the time, and the local newspaper said so in its wedding announcement. Aunt Julia, Uncle Earl, and Roy Earl are all buried in the Fielding Cemetery.

...In the early 1980s, I spent a day in Grahn, finding remnants of Mom's first school, Rattlesnake. I had to stop three times and ask for directions to the old school. Of course it was in ruins, but some of the old stones were still there. I brought back one stone and had Mom's name engraved on it. She was touched when I gave it to her for Christmas. I still have that stone.

...Everyone knew that Esther was a great cook. She attracted a lot of people to the dining table for many years. Breakfast was her specialty. I think that Esther's breakfast was big enough to last Preacher the whole day. Eggs, bacon, sausage, drop biscuits, gravy, and fried apples. Then came the oatmeal. I was always amazed at how often she fixed that meal and how regularly Papa ate it. Harlan also loved that meal, and so did I, although I could barely walk afterwards.

...In 1965, Dad and I went to see the movie "The Longest Day" about the Normandy invasion. As a history buff, I knew well Operation Overlord, the beaches, troop movements, etc. Dad, who landed on Omaha beach six hours after the first wave of troops, knew nothing then and still cared to know nothing about the strategy behind the invasion. I realized that he, along with thousands of other soldiers, was just doing what he was told to do while trying to stay alive.

...Harlan and I watched TV quite a lot while we lived at Enterprise and Soldier. Saturday mornings were Roy Rogers, Sky King, and lots of cartoons. I remember 1956, when I was 9 years old, watching Estes Kefauver deliver his acceptance speech at the Democratic National Convention and telling Mom and Dad I liked Ike better. We also had a TV in Hayward, but I only remember playing with cars under the kitchen table while everybody else watched wrestling.

"We were the first couple at Hayward to have a television set, and therefore, we had a lot of company. One Saturday afternoon I invited Donnie and Lloyd Tackett with their wives to watch television and play some cards. They were having beer, and it was fun until the two brothers got into a fight. They went out the front door, and Cooge was trying to separate them when one of them pulled a knife and Cooge's arm was cut. That broke up the fight and I drove him to Morehead for a doctor. We lied about how he received the cut because we were afraid it would have to be reported."

...At Soldier, we had a dog named Duffy. We were getting into Mom's car to go to school one morning, and Duffy got hit by a car right in front of our eyes. Mom carried Duffy's limp body to the garage and we went off to school. I was devastated all day, but surprised in the evening when we got home and Duffy greeted us. When we moved, we left Duffy with the house's new owner. On one of our early return trips to Kentucky we went to see Duffy. We were crushed when the owner said that Duffy had chased the neighbor's chickens and had to be shot.

...It was not unusual for a teacher at Soldier to teach two classes in one room. Mom taught me in the 3rd grade, and the next year I moved over to the other side of the room as a 4th grader. I remember once Mom telling me to sit down in class and I refused, really fronting her off in front of the other students. I think she took this personally, so she had no option other than to turn my ass red. Dad was my best friend for the next two weeks.

...Talk about busting your behind. Once, at Hayward, I took a crayon and made a drawing on the bedroom wallpaper. I blamed it on Harlan, who was barely old enough to hold a crayon, much less make an intelligent drawing. Mom went out back and got a switch and tore into my behind. The switch she cut was from a Milkweed plant that we soon found out I was allergic to. My whole body bloated up like a balloon. As adults we laughed over it for decades, and I held it over her head as cruel and unusual punishment of a minor. I think Mom learned her discipline from Preacher.

"Dad came home in the middle of the day and went straight to the small peach tree on the back lawn. We knew that one of us was to be whipped. Without explanation, he picked up Jack and started whipping him. I threw myself on top of Jack and Dad whipped both of us. It seems that Dad had gone down to pay our charge account bill at Rayburn's and there was a flashlight charged to him. Jack had bought the light and paid for it. Jack Rayburn remembered later that he had paid, and they apologized; but that did not save our backs."

...I have more memories of Hayward than Harlan. I remember Dad won a pig in a poker game. We kept that pig for a while and fattened

Revenue Form 740-S   · Page 4

KENTUCKY INDIVIDUAL INCOME TAX RETURN 1956
(For Kentucky Residents Only)

Read Instructions on Page 8 Carefully

1. Print Name **Ruth Davis**

Print Address

City **Soldier** State **Ky.**

2. Social Security Number — First Name of Spouse **Harlan**

3. TAX CREDITS: Check blocks which apply. Check for spouse if she/he had no income or her/his income is included in this return.

A. Tax credit for ... ☒ Self ☐ Spouse
65 or over at end of taxable year ... ☐ Self ☐ Spouse
Blind at end of taxable year ... ☐ Self ☐ Spouse

B. List dependents **1 (myself)**

C. Total blocks checked plus dependents listed **1**

4. Total wages (see instructions) ... $ **2,156.74**
5. Excludable "Sick Pay" (see instructions) ... **217.91**
6. Balance (Item 4 minus Item 5) ... **1938.83**
7. Other Income (see instructions) ... **0.0**
8. Federal tax refunded in 1956 ... **0.0**
9. Gross Income (Add Items 6, 7 and 8) $ **1938.83**
10. Federal tax paid during 1956 ... **298.70**
11. Adjusted Gross Income (9 minus 10) ... $ **1640.13**
12. Enter tax from Table, page 7 ... $ **17.84**
13. Enter Kentucky tax withheld ... **22.26**
14. TAX DUE (Item 12 minus Item 13) ... $
15. REFUND DUE (Item 13 minus Item 12) $ **4.42**

I certify that this is a true and correct return.
Ruth Davis 4/5/57
Signature of Taxpayer (wife also sign if joint return)   Date

him up, until one day someone came and shot the pig. The neighbors helped with the butchering, and by the end of the day we had sausage and hams hanging in the smokehouse.

...All the elementary schools in Carter County competed with each other in volleyball and basketball. Soldier had the only indoor gym, in a separate building next to the school. There were pot belly stoves in each of the four corners and a small stage at the end. Once a year, all the schools came to Soldier for the Carter County elementary school version of March Madness. There were no classes on that day, and for those in the first four or five grades it was a free day to play.

...Clyde Fultz, a second grade classmate of mine, certainly knew how to pee. He peed in the bed during my first classmate overnighter. I also remember the Carter County Health Nurse coming for an annual urine screening at each school, and we were requested to bring in a urine sample. Mom had Harlan and I fill our small cups that morning. Clyde came walking up that steep school hill with about a gallon of urine in the family chamber pot. He told the nurse he had some difficulty getting that much pee in such a short time period.

1950 chamber pot

...Harlan and I learned to play cards with Miss Flori Carpenter and her husband Everett. Everett was a carpenter in name and deed. He helped Mom and Dad with wiring at Hayward, and helped them acquire appliances that were hard to get after the war. Flori and Everett shared their home in Soldier with a man named Bud. Mom, Dad, Harlan and I would visit them on occasion and spend evenings playing 500 card Rummy with them.

...One night while living in Soldier, Mom didn't know where Dad was. She suspected he was playing poker somewhere, so she put Harlan and I in the car and we went to find him. We found him in the back of the gas station in Enterprise drinking, swapping lies, and playing cards with a bunch of guys. Mom roared in there like a lion and jerked him out like a puppy on a leash. There must have been something else going on between them, since when we returned home they got into one of the deepest conversations I have ever witnessed between them. Harlan and I were awake for this, although I'm sure

Mom and Dad wished we weren't. I remember Dad getting real remorseful about a hunting accident he had years ago. He broke down crying and Mom put her arms around him. The lion and the leash both disappeared. Although Harlan and I never learned any details about that accident, that night was the most emotional I ever saw Dad.

...In the early summer of 1959, the Mayflower truck pulled up to our house in Soldier, packed our things, and took off for Mansfield. On our last night living in Kentucky, Mom, Dad, Harlan and I stayed at Papa's and Esther's. We got up the next morning and headed down Route 174 for the last time as Kentucky residents. Harlan and I cried.

Visiting relatives in Mansfield

Tying It All Together

Different generations see the world differently.

Our ancestors are a link to our past and a window to our future.Many family members find it interesting to learn the history of their family. The real challenge is to figure out what makes a particular family member tick at a certain time and place in history.

As a child living in Hayward, Enterprise, and Soldier, I certainly didn't understand with any depth my family's beliefs, emotions, and preferences. As an adult, I can only take what memories I have, written notes from Mom, scratchings on the backs of old pictures, stories from living family elders, and add my own remembered truths in order to make sense out of the Davis/Hall lives decades ago.

Life is lived in people's experiences and perceptions. It is a story told through the eyes of those that live it. Here is my stab at the Davis/Hall family story.

1855-1929

The Civil War was the greatest American crisis in terms of causalities – over 600,000. Daniel Davis was nine years old when it ended, old enough to know that something big had just happened in his childhood.

Kentucky was a border state that had plenty of divided families and politicians. Daniel could not have avoided the "bloody-shirt" veterans spewing hatred toward the South, or the Reconstructionists who just wanted to get back to some form of normalcy.

Mom Davis

Daniel came of age at a time when a hostile world on the battlefield started to shift towards industrialism and commercialism. The adults in Daniel's world were starting to seek their fortunes in steel, railroads, mines, and oil wells. It was a time when political corruption and labor disputes erupted.

Carter County started its makeover in the 1880s. At that time, its iron ore industry of the past 60 years was being replaced by the discovery of a unique type of fire clay that made fire bricks to supply the Industrial Revolution. Olive Hill, the sleepy little stagecoach stop on the Midland Trail, was about to become a Saturday night town. Morehead was going to start a college just as soon as the Rowan County War got rid of the Tollivers.

It was the 1880s discovery of this "Olive Hill District" fire clay that probably lured Daniel Davis to Carter County to work and seek his fortune. It was here that he met Jenny, a young woman whose generation found themselves alienated as children and alone as adults. It is easy to see how a Jenny would fall for a Pied Piper like Dan.

The commercial activity that attracted Daniel Davis could also have attracted Daniel Boone Hall to take a look at Carter County after the turn of the century. Daniel Boone Hall's childhood was somewhere around Morgan County. As a twenty-something adult, he did what was considered the right thing to do for his generation, marching off to Cuba to "Remember the Maine."

Daniel Boone Hall and Stewart

I only knew Daniel Boone Hall as an elder. He always appeared statesman-like, with a "been there, done that" attitude. My guess is that he saw himself as half a step above everyone else. Maybe his nickname should have been Preacher instead of Stewart. Probably no one alive knows how his liaison with Emily Perry occurred. However, generationally, they are alike, and when two likes get together, they can produce a Stewart Henry.

Emily, abandoned by Daniel Boone, married twice-divorced James Fielding, a man 15 years her senior and already a father of eight children. Together, Emily and Jim produced six children. Stewart, a half-brother to all the other kids, was probably well-protected by his mother and influenced heavily by his stepfather.

The world was moving faster than ever during Stewart's childhood. Internationally, there was turmoil in Europe. Nationally, there were rapid technological changes, immigrants were pouring into the East and moving West, and the labor movement was raising hell like a weasel in a henhouse. Locally, Stewart saw new brick plants being constructed, rail transportation expanding, and limestone being mined. Stewart was a builder and a doer, and he was in a good place at a good time in Carter County.

One movement that impacted Stewart throughout his adult life was women's suffrage, one of the great social movements in American history. Stewart was 20 years old when the 19th amendment was signed, giving women the right to vote.

Emily was the benefactor of early women's activism as she started raising a bastard child alone in 1900. Stella had the right to vote when Stewart wooed and married her. I think Stella was sly as a fox and mentally stronger than she was physically. Behind closed doors I think she was Stewart's equal, a persona Stewart probably didn't wish the public to see.

Ruth Mary

The first of Stella and Stewart's children, Ruth Mary, my Mom, was to become as independent as a Gypsy. Three other daughters followed. Julia, Stewart's half-sister, was a strong advocate for education whose voice haunted Stewart to see that those children got a good education. And Esther? Esther became the recognized thread that Stewart and the rest of the family came to depend upon. She did it quietly and over time, but there was no doubt as to her inner strength.

I chuckle to think of all the women's issues Stewart faced as an adult, and picture Daniel Boone Hall constantly whispering advice in Stewart's ear. And Jenny Rose, Daniel Davis' new bride? I don't think she got the women's suffrage memo, as she birthed six children from 1911 to 1923. What a song Daniel must have sung.

1929

The picture in 1929 was pretty clear. The Fielding/Hall and Davis families were not yet related. If they knew each other, it was just in passing or playing poker.

Stewart and Stella's family was well on its way to being complete. Four of the six children were already born, while one, Billy, had passed away. Stewart was busy building and working and Stella was at home. Trains were passing through Enterprise east and west, transporting firebricks and people. Daniel and Jenny's children were all born, the oldest being 18 and the youngest six. Daniel was roaming and Jenny was at home.

Internationally, World War I was over and the United States, like Mighty Mouse, had saved the day. Millions of Europeans were killed, but only a few thousand US troops. The war didn't seem to affect Carter County all that much.

At the end of the war in 1918, the nation's eyes had turned inward. To be sure, there were some moralists trying to impose their value system on the country, and a lot of people thought we were going to hell in a hand basket. Overall, though, happy days were here again. Skirting prohibition became fun. Flappers flapped through the Roaring 20s. Movies talked. Lots of new black automobiles were seen everywhere. Babe Ruth was a hero. Few cared that the haves were getting more and the have-nots were getting less.

Times were also good in Carter County. Matthew Sellers had brought Olive Hill some fame, and Olive Hill had a baseball team and a new school overlooking the city. Education was on the move. Morehead College was growing and the Moonlight Schools had bolstered adult education. Train carloads of firebricks were lining everything from railroad engines to blast furnaces throughout the country. Lawton, Enterprise, Hayward, Soldier, and Haldeman were humming.

Then, the 1929 stock market crash changed everything.

The next crisis

The cycles of history usually change gradually, but this was not the case in 1929. Overnight, the stock market crash ushered out a decades-old financial boom and ushered in America's next great crisis, The Great Depression and World War II. It had been 69 years since the last crisis, The Civil War.

The Great Depression was a nationwide economic failure. It caused massive unemployment, homelessness, and hopelessness for everyone. Every American was impacted, including everyone in Carter County and the Fielding/Hall and Davis families.

Daniel Davis died in 1933, leaving Jenny with six children. Dad was now in his early twenties and working at the Hayward plant. He took it upon himself to help support Jenny and his siblings. Stella passed away in 1935, leaving Stewart with five children, ages two through nine. Stewart, in his early thirties, made a crucial decision at a crucial time to try and keep the family together. This generation, born between 1900 and 1924, later named the G.I. Generation, would now start to show its mettle by rolling up its sleeves and demonstrating a no-nonsense, get-it-done attitude.

Generation scholars have generally agreed that the birth years of 1925 through 1946 created a different generation than that born between 1900 and 1924. To understand why just one year can be so decisive in generational characteristics, you only have to look closer at the Fielding/Hall family at the time of the 1929 stock market crash.

Ruth Mary, my Mom, was the only family child born before 1925, with the other five children all being born after 1925. During the Great Depression Mom ranged in age from six to sixteen, old enough to have comparable memories of better times. Jack and Margarette did not reach their teenage years during the Depression. Kathaleen and Betty did not even reach the age of ten. Life was tough for a lot of folks and they remembered happier days. But, for Kathaleen and Betty, this was the only life they knew.

The generation of Jack, Marge, Kathaleen, and Betty was named The Silent Generation. Both the G.I Generation and the Silent Generation experienced The Great Depression and World War II. However, Mom's G.I. Generation became actively involved in the crisis while the other siblings, The Silent Generation, were still growing up during the crisis.

Cooge, my Dad, fought in the war at age 31. Ruth, my Mom, started teaching at age 16 because the men were away fighting. She even worked on land mines in a defense plant one summer. The G.I. Generation set the tone and direction for the country for decades to come and the Silent Generation became the sensitive helpmates. This helps explain why Mom ruffled a lot more feathers throughout her life than Jack, Marge, Kathaleen, and Betty. Although the two generations are identified separately, they both were civic-oriented and worked together for the common good.

Post World War II

The twin 16-year crisis of The Depression and World War II left indelible impressions on everyone. Many people believed that life would return to how it was before the war and the Depression, but this was not so. Returning veterans got married, had kids, moved into nice homes, stayed family-centered, and got productive jobs. A new historical cycle began with VJ Day and it didn't end until the early 60s. For almost 20 years, the G.I. and Silent Generations got busy building strong institutions and bringing order and harmony to society.

Dad returned to the Hayward plant, while Mom continued to teach. They met shortly after the war, got married and had two early Baby Boomer sons, Michael, me, in 1947 and Harlan in 1949. Some of Mom and Dad's siblings were now young adults, while others were approaching

Superman and Batman

adulthood. They were marrying and moving on, some north to where the post-war industrialization provided greater job opportunities.

Esther and Stewart were married at the start of the War, and post-war found them raising Patty and Allen in Enterprise. Daniel Boone Hall had returned from his Lewis and Clark Pacific journey and started shuffling between families in Carter and Morgan counties for food and shelter.

Harlan and I, as well as all our post-war cousins, were well-nurtured in our childhood. We were labeled "Spock babies" after Dr. Benjamin Spock. We were coaxed, not threatened by our parents, and our childhood, compared to our parents' childhood, was very secure. Our parents had just come back from the apocalypse, and their children would not come close to experiencing what they had experienced.

Our future was very promising as television opened our eyes to life's banquet. In fact, we were influenced a lot by what we saw on television. Simple plots and happy endings occurred in half-hour black and white time periods. We started a pattern of identifying heroes, a pattern that would stick with us through adulthood. It seemed that America was focused on us 24/7. The world was at our fingertips, while the generations that spawned us thought we would obediently follow the yellow brick road they built to a world they had only dreamed of. That was not to be.

1959

Things had started to change in Carter County leading up to 1959. Northern industry that had previously made bombs and tanks in the war rapidly mobilized to turn out stoves and refrigerators. Mansfield Ohio's Westinghouse plant employed thousands of workers. New technology was appearing quickly, including a new way to manufacture steel. This new technology, combined with the Carter County fire clay being depleted, resulted in many Carter Countians out-migrating to northern jobs.

The Hayward brick plant that Dad had worked at since 1926 closed down in 1957. Dad and Mom made the decision to move our family to Mansfield, a hotbed for jobs at the time. By then, many of our aunts, uncles, and cousins were already living away from the communities of Route 174. Little did we recognize that the "good times" post World War II cycle of history was coming to a close, and another one was about to start – the 1960s and 70s.

"Me" to "We"

Although each of us is born into a generation, it doesn't mean that we have to like it. Many of my generation, born between 1946 and 1964, totally wrapped themselves in the warm boomer generation blanket. Rebellion against our parents' generation was commonplace. The Summer of Love. Days of Rage. Woodstock. Sit ins. Vietnam War marches. Kent State.

I am guilty of being work-and-goal-oriented and highly independent throughout my adult life. Yes, I owned a leisure suit; however, my draft card did not get burned and I never participated in the rebellious acts against the previous generation. My music choice remained in the late 50s and early 60s, not the 70s' flower child songs.

There is no doubting that my 77-million-strong baby boomer generation questioned and then impacted the values so well-defined by my parents' generation. My generation created a spiritual awakening. We are, as a generation, an idealistic "me" generation as opposed to the civic "we" generation. We took control of this country at the 1968 Democratic Convention, and didn't let go until the presidential election of 2008. We are still clawing and scratching as we reluctantly accept the new rules, but we will have no choice but to obediently fall into line like our elders have always done.

The "We" generation is in charge now – the Millennials. They are just gathering up a head of steam. Conventional wisdom says this generation, the generation of my grandchildren, will return to an era of civic duty and teamwork. Their value system will resemble the value system of the generation that won War World II, my parent's generation.

When my parents were growing up in the late 1920s, no one was calling their generation the greatest generation ever. They were not being told they were great kids. They earned their reputation through the double crisis of The Great Depression and World War II. My grandchildren's generation will have the same opportunity as the G.I. Generation, born 1900-1924.

For 500 years now, the cycles of history have arrived on schedule. If you were sitting on Mt. Olympus in Greek mythology, you could see the American Revolution crisis coming. You could look forward one lifetime and see the Civil War, and in another lifetime see The Great Depression and World War II.

Unfortunately, one lifetime away from our last crisis, The Depression and World War II, lies the next great crisis. It's scheduled to arrive around 2025, maybe a little sooner. It will undoubtedly be global in scale.

The current mindset is that our country is unraveling. We are pessimistic about our future and the American Dream appears to be just that, a dream. We are adrift. The world seems to be crumbling before our eyes.

The truth is, this has all happened before. Today's pessimism is similar to the feelings Americans had in the 1920s as they danced their way to the stock market crash. The 1850s before the Civil War were torn apart by sectionalism and slavery. Preceding the American Revolution were long debates among the colonists about our relationship with England. It's the same underlying discontent as today, just different details.

In all previous crises, the "We" generation, like my parent's generation, and the current Millennial generation, have put out the fires. The "We" generation has always been the generation on the front line to resolve the crisis. In all likelihood, my grandchildren's generation will rise to the yet unknown crisis. In this cycle of history, it will be their time to step up.

Can the crisis be averted? History says no. You cannot eliminate winter because you want to go from fall to spring.

A look back at the Davis/Hall family tree will not find anyone who left fingerprints on the world. However, let's hope their fingerprints will be all over my grandchildren's generation.

And, let's hope the places they grew up are as meaningful to them as The Ghost Towns of 174 were to my family. These six small communities today may be devoid of a discernible future, but they remain anchored in the hearts and minds of thousands of Kentucky families.

About the author

For over 40 years, Willie (Michael) Davis has been an educator and marketing communications expert, giving individuals and businesses "a real chance" to be the best they can be. He has simplified the complex world of marketing for many small businesses. In addition, he has developed and implemented innovative criminal justice programs at both the state and local corrections level. Willie and his business partner, Dr. Samantha Kurtz, are currently developing an innovative approach to reducing recidivism for ex-offenders and a unique resiliency program for disenfranchised populations. You can learn more about him at www.peoplelution.biz and contact him at willie@peoplelution.biz. Willie lives with his wife Karen in Mansfield, Ohio, and has two daughters, Jami and Erin, and five grandchildren.

Willie's brother, Harlan, lives in Knoxville, Tennessee with his wife Cindy. They have three grown children, Molly, Adam and Greg.